COLIN G. MAGGS

A 1930S CHILDHOOD

FROM CONKER FIGHTS TO COAL FIRES

The History Press

First published 2022

The History Press
97 St George's Place, Cheltenham,
Gloucestershire, GL50 3QB
www.thehistorypress.co.uk

British Library Cataloguing in Publication Data.
A catalogue record for this book is available from the British Library.

ISBN 978 0 7509 9724 9

Typesetting and origination by The History Press
Printed and bound in Great Britain by TJ Books Limited, Padstow, Cornwall.

MIX
Paper from
responsible sources
FSC® C013056

Trees for LYfe

CONTENTS

Sitting on Grandad's knee. (Courtesy of Stephen Dodds)

INTRODUCTION

The 1930s! What an exciting decade in which a child could grow up! The world really was becoming modern: internal combustion-powered vehicles were superseding horse transport; open-top buses and trams, comparable to the outside of a stage coach, were being replaced with covered tops. Cars were of the saloon type for year-round use, rather than the earlier open variety which could only be used in good weather. Air travel was even possible. Streamlining was all the rage: it made sense for rail, road and air travel, but to create a modern appearance, it was also applied to household articles and, similarly, modern architecture displayed smooth, uncluttered lines.

The decade marked the heyday of the steam locomotive because, later, due to the Second World War, there would be little development in the forties, while in the fifties the change would be made to electric or diesel–electric propulsion.

In those ten years, life in the home changed. To be up to date, you lit your home by electricity, not gas or oil. Plastic in the form of Bakelite was being used to make various objects. It was a time when many new homes were built, creating suburbs around cities, and many people, with the help of building societies, became homeowners. It was the wage-earner's ambition to provide a home for his family, probably semi-detached and preferably with a garage, for they might even be able to afford a car on hire purchase. The thirties' building boom saw the norm of a semi-detached house with a front garden being the favoured design, rather than the terraced houses which had been preferred earlier in the century, with just a garden at the rear. Towns were expanding so much that villages on their perimeter were absorbed as suburbs.

At the start of the decade, radios were rare, but by its end the majority of households owned one. Methods of heating were beginning to change. Most homes had coal fires, but gas and electric fires, although more expensive, were useful in spring and autumn when you only needed heat in the evening. Coal fires meant that there was always the risk of smog (smoky fog) on still days when there was no wind to disperse the smoke.

Although horse transport was dying out, it was still very much used in the countryside for carrying people in traps, and for many jobs on the farm. The standard of living was improving and many more people could afford a week's holiday.

The effects of the First World War were still visible: it was common to see wounded servicemen who were blind or lacking limbs since artificial limbs were not readily available; other ex-servicemen were tucked away out of sight because they were suffering mental health problems. There was a preponderance of spinsters and widows because of the number of men who had been killed in the war and were therefore not available to be husbands.

Although from 1933 it was very obvious that Nazi Germany was stealing territory from other countries, we in Great Britain were very reluctant to go to war; the memories and results of the previous one, with its great loss of lives, being all too recent.

Britain was still very imperialist – the empire, which was coloured pink on the map, covered a quarter of the world and we liked to think that we were a very important power. Due to the expense, few people travelled abroad and so adopted an insular attitude believing that other countries did things in strange, odd and perhaps foolish ways.

People living in the 1930s lived more content lives because they had lower expectations: they were satisfied with a roof, warmth and food. Other things such as a radio or a visit to the cinema were viewed as luxuries and very much a bonus. People sang and whistled in the streets because they were happy; they did it for joy, not cash.

ACKNOWLEDGEMENTS

Thanks are due to Dr Sheila Barry, Margaret and Alan Dudeney, Phill Martin, Newton Tainsh and Shean Whyte for help received, and especial thanks to Colin Roberts for checking and improving the text. Thanks to Stephen Dodds for supplementary photographs.

Dressing in your best.
(Courtesy of Stephen Dodds)

One

HOME LIFE

In the thirties, there was more disparity than you see today. For most people, money was very tight, with an average wage of about £2 10s. With care, you had just about enough to live on, but certainly none to spare for luxuries. Should you be out of work and 'on the dole', you received £1 7s 3d a week plus 2s for each child. Children's pocket money was about a penny a week – enough to buy a packet of sweets, but you needed 2d for a bar of chocolate and 6d to 1s for most Dinky Toys. It might have been possible to get a job delivering either morning or evening papers, helping a local tradesman, or singing in a church choir.

The standard of housing varied greatly. In England and Wales, many factory workers lived in terrace housing, while those in Scotland occupied tenements. These were usually close to the place of employment so offered the advantage of easy and quick travel, but the disadvantage of being close to the noise, dirt and smoke of the factories.

Terrace and tenement families dreamed of owning a semi-detached house, perhaps even with a garage. Modern homes had metal window frames which closed firmly and did not rattle like sash windows, and some of the really up-to-date bay windows actually had curved glass on the corners. The railways encouraged house building, realising that it would mean an increase in season ticket sales and also income from the carriage of coal and goods needed by those relocating. The Metropolitan Railway's publicity department created the term 'Metro-land' to encourage the building of housing estates alongside its line, which extended as far as Verney Junction in Buckinghamshire, 50½ miles from London. The Southern Railway encouraged house building by electrifying many of its lines in the London area. It produced posters bearing such phrases as 'Live in Kent and be Content' and 'Live in Surrey, Free from Worry'.

Certainly, those who could afford a home in the suburbs enjoyed better living conditions, but had the disadvantage of spending time and money commuting. Travel could be by foot, cycle, bus, tram, trolleybus or train, but not usually by car, as if you could afford a car, it was kept for leisure use at weekends or evenings, not to travel to and from work. As an economy, a significant proportion of private car drivers did not tax their car for the first quarter of the year because the weather in those three months did not generally encourage outings.

The author and his mother in 1933 outside his home which was built the previous year. Sited on a bend, the plot of land was wedge-shaped so, unlike most houses of the era, the two main downstairs rooms and the two main bedrooms were at the front, the small bedroom being at the rear. (G. T. Maggs)

If you ran short of money, you might have used a pawn shop, perhaps taking your best suit along on Monday, being loaned a sum of money for it and then redeeming it the following Saturday. Although this was not really a wise way to live because the pawnbroker had to earn a living and you had to pay for the loan, it was the only way some could manage.

If space was at a premium, families might have had to cook, eat and live in one room, but, if possible, these three activities were carried out in three separate rooms. The lounge might have been kept for special occasions, such as Christmas and funerals.

The dining room was furnished with a table, often with an expanding leaf for when entertaining visitors; upright chairs, perhaps with arms for use by Mother and Father; and a sideboard in which to keep the best china and glasses, with drawers for tablecloths, napkins and special cutlery, again for when entertaining visitors. When set for a meal, a table in that era was considered quite naked without a covering. On the sideboard was a fruit bowl and a stand of place mats. If the radio was not kept in the dining room, there might have been a loudspeaker connected to the wireless. The fireplace had a set of fire irons and a clock stood on the mantelpiece.

The sitting room had a suite of settee and two matching chairs, all in fabric or leather, the settee perhaps being capable of being adapted as a bed for overnight visitors. There would also have been a few easy chairs and a table or two on which to put books and flowers. The room may also have had a bureau, bookcase, coal scuttle, fire-iron stand, and a clock on the mantelpiece. For the family's entertainment it may well have contained a piano, radio and gramophone. Ashtrays were plentiful around the house as most people smoked and, as there were no air fresheners, windows had to be opened to get rid of the smell.

There were two types of gramophone: a mechanical one, which was fairly portable, but you would not want to carry it very far. This was operated by a hand-wound motor and relied on a horn to magnify the sound, but later models had the horn distorted and cunningly placed below the turntable. Other gramophones were electric. Both types used metal needles which were supposed to be replaced for each record. The hand-operated gramophones could also use very economical wooden needles which could be sharpened using a special tool. All gramophones used records which had to be played at 78 revolutions per minute. If an electric motor had been lubricated with thick grease, it took some time for it to warm up before the table rotated at the correct speed. The records were brittle and it was all too easy to crack one if it were dropped or sat on. Should you be able to afford it, the real luxury of the decade was the radiogram, which combined a wireless and gramophone; it even allowed you to pile several records on at a time and would actually change them automatically!

Whether in the dining room or front room, there was quite likely to be a piano. In this decade, more children learnt to play a piano than do today. Apart from being a useful accomplishment and entertainment for the child, the skill could be very useful for making friends or perhaps even getting a job in the future. If two people of equal ability were seeking a teaching post, the one who could play the piano was more likely to be offered it. Falling out of use during the era, because of the much more adaptable gramophone, was the pianola. At first glance it appeared to be an ordinary upright piano, but wider from back to front. A roll of music could be purchased which consisted of a card with punched holes. You inserted this into the pianola and pressed a pedal to generate wind which blew through those holes and sounded particular piano keys, making it look as if you were playing the piano without moving your hands. In addition to playing these rolls, it could be played like an ordinary piano.

As there was only one radio in the house, everyone in the family would gather round to listen to the popular programmes and had to listen when it was actually being broadcast for there was no domestic means of recording a programme in those days. The BBC was held in awe as it only used speakers who enunciated the Queen's English. It broadcast entertainment and news programmes and was really the only means of telling the correct time. If you missed the time signal, you would ask someone, 'Please can you tell me the correct wireless time?' The term 'wireless' was used because, unlike the telephone, it did not need to be connected by wire.

At the very end of the decade, television became available, but only to those living in the London area and at a price out of the reach of many. The picture quality was quite poor and grainy.

The kitchen had a sink, usually only one draining board, a plate rack and cooker. This would probably be gas, this being cheaper than electricity. If you could afford it, rather than using matches to light the gas, you would have a gas pistol. Some people, especially those living in the country, cooked from an oven beside the fire. Others used a Primus stove which was started by methylated spirits evaporating paraffin, which was then put under pressure, and it looked and acted much as a town-gas ring.

There would be cupboards for storing crockery and food, while for wash days there would be a galvanised tub with gas ring below. When the laundry had boiled sufficiently and was deemed clean, it was lifted out with wooden tongs. Products such as Persil, Rinso and Oxydol could be used to help the cleansing process, while another useful product was Eezall, advertised as 'What granny used to use'. It was manufactured just a few miles from my home and one day, out on a cycle ride, I spotted the factory where it was made and was surprised to see how small the building was – not much larger than a domestic garage, which was surprising given Eezall was a nationwide brand.

A mangle was used to squeeze as much water out of the laundry as possible before it was hung on the line. A child was often asked to turn the mangle while an adult fed the laundry between the rollers and it was always tempting to try to turn the handle quickly and see if you could squeeze the adult's hands. The two rollers were kept together by a strong spring; before use, the spring was screwed down and after use it was relaxed. Scotland had wash houses owned by the local council.

The washing line was outside and, if it was long and slack, was supported by a clothes prop in the shape of a long, forked stick. If it rained, you may have had a framework which could be lowered by pulleys from the kitchen ceiling and then hoisted up for the washing to dry indoors, but this created a damp odour. An alternative was to place the washing in front of the fire on a clothes-horse, taking great care that the garments did not go up in flames. As everyone did their washing on

Monday, it was acknowledged that no one was anti-social enough to light a bonfire in the garden that day. As smokeless zones were still far in the future, bonfires were an enjoyable means of disposing of your garden waste and any other combustible rubbish. There were many possibilities: you could pretend you were firing a railway locomotive or use it to bake potatoes, and, in winter, keep warm all at the same time.

When the washing was dry, it had to be ironed and many homes still used flat irons, either heated beside a coal fire or on a gas ring. You needed at least two irons: one to use while the other was getting hot; but very modern homes owned an electric iron, often plugged into an overhead light. If you didn't have much money, you would do all the washing and ironing yourself, but the more affluent sent the larger items, such as sheets, to the laundry, which would collect them by van, wash and iron them, and then deliver them home.

There seemed to be many more flies about in those days and fly-papers were a common sight, especially in kitchens. Often suspended from a light in the ceiling, the strips of paper were about 2 feet in length and 4 inches wide, covered with an arsenic-based adhesive substance that flies stuck to. This led to detective stories being written at the time about people extracting the chemical from the fly-papers to use as poison.

Mice could be another health hazard and were dealt with by a back-break trap. This consisted of a wooden platform, U-shaped piece of strong wire and a spring. The bait, usually a piece of cheese, was placed at one end of the trap and, when the mouse took the cheese, this triggered the spring which caused the strong metal wire to snap down and break the mouse's back, killing it immediately.

The main downstairs rooms were heated by open coal fires which generally burnt all day and, when unattended, had a wire fireguard in front to prevent sparks flying out and setting the room alight. If you lived in the country, you might well have had a wood fire because you could get your children to collect the fuel free of charge. The act of sawing the branches into short lengths was another means of generating heat to keep warm. House-proud women liked to black lead the grate so that it looked gleaming and well cared for.

The dining room fire might have had a back-boiler for heating water, or an oven on one side of the fire. There may have been cast-iron discs on each side of the fire which could be swung over in front of it to heat a kettle or saucepan, all of which were very economical.

Maintaining a coal fire was time-consuming. It had to be set up, often by older children, with a base of crumpled newspaper, kindling wood and coal, the ashes having been removed without spreading too much dust in the air.

A match would set the newspaper alight and hopefully set the wood on fire, which in turn would ignite the coal. If the fire did not draw, a very exciting solution was available to grown-ups, but was far too dangerous for children to try. A broadsheet newspaper would be held tightly across the fireplace, as close to the fire as possible. This would restrict the flow of air so that it could only come from beneath the fire and pass through to make the coal burn well. The danger was that, sooner or later, the newspaper would go up in flames and had to be thrust on to the fire quickly before it caught the house alight. This method of getting a fire going was great fun to watch, but a less exciting way was to use a pair of bellows.

Unless a fire was needed for hot water (for example, in spring and autumn when it may only have been chilly in the evening), rather than go to the trouble of lighting a fire and then having to clean it, re-lay it and make it smart by polishing with black lead, some households used a gas or electric fire.

A coal fire was splendid for toasting crumpets or bread on the end of a toasting fork, which perhaps you made at senior school from wire bent to form a handle and three prongs. It was always fun watching someone else do the toasting because there was always an excellent chance that the slice of bread would fall off into the fire and go up in flames – always good for a laugh.

Coal or wood fires generated soot, which was combustible. This meant that about once a year there would be the excitement of the sweep's visit. It was essential to have your chimneys swept because a chimney fire would lead to a fine because it could easily lead to the whole house catching fire. A chimney fire was very obvious because it created so much black smoke and an obnoxious smell.

The sweep, covered in soot, arrived on his bike and was actually invited by your mother to come into her nice clean rooms – if you were as dirty as he was, you would have been ordered to have a bath!

Mother had already made preparations and pushed the furniture back from the fireplace and covered it with an old sheet. The sweep poked a brush up the chimney, adding more rods as it ascended and then you rushed outside to see it appear through the chimney pot. As the sweep steadily withdrew the brushes, soot would fall down the chimney and into his sack, not into the room. Mum would be anxious that, as the sweep left, he didn't rub the sack or dirty clothes against her nice clean paintwork or wallpaper.

The sweep would then ask whether we wanted the soot – it was useful for preventing slugs from eating plants. I noticed that the sweep had white teeth and was told that this was because he cleaned his teeth with soot. I just couldn't understand how cleaning with something black could make them white any more than I could understand how putting a blue bag in with the white washing could make it whiter.

Modern houses, or modernised homes, had electric light, but many older houses still had gas lights. Homes in the country with no mains electricity or gas supply relied on oil or paraffin lights, but if you were really up to date, you would use gas from a cylinder. Some paraffin lamps were of the Tilley variety which vapourised the paraffin and gave a brighter light than was given by a wick burning paraffin. The railway companies were great users of Tilley lamps.

Many houses which had electricity at this time were only wired for lighting and if you needed current for any other purpose, say an electric iron or vacuum cleaner, you took out a bulb and plugged in the appliance. My mother powered her Hoover via the light above my bed.

One evening, I was just drifting off to sleep when there was a thump on my pillow. I was scared stiff, believing that a criminal had punched the pillow beside my head. For safety, I dived deep down under the bedclothes.

After a few moments, realising that I was still alive, I warily felt around with my hand and touched something round and warm – the light bulb had not been securely inserted and had fallen from its fitting!

Homes which had electric sockets had the round-pin type, with either two or three holes. Often, schools did not have wall sockets and many teachers plugged a kettle into the electric light to boil their water for a cup of tea.

Homes which did not have electricity, or could not afford a vacuum cleaner, used a carpet sweeper. This was an appliance with a long handle and, when pushed, round brushes picked up dirt and rubbish from the floor and stored it before you emptied it into the dustbin.

Homes with a mains gas supply usually had a brass tap in each room. From this, a flexible metal tube with rubber at each end could be used to connect the tap to whatever gas appliance was required at that particular moment: perhaps a fire, a ring for boiling a kettle, or a gas poker for getting the coal fire started. It was only much later that it was standard practice for the appliance to be permanently fixed in place.

The gas used then was not North Sea gas but a product made at the gas works. Coal was heated in retorts but not given any oxygen, so the gas given off by the coal did not burn but was stored in a gas holder. This was a very large iron cylinder with its lower end sealed by water so it could rise and fall as consumers used its contents. After the gas had been extracted from the coal, coke, a smokeless fuel, remained. Early in the twentieth century, all towns and even some large villages had their own gas works, but in the thirties, economies were made by larger gas companies taking over and closing the smaller ones, laying connecting mains and thus creating a grid over the whole country.

Children might have had their own bedroom, but often had to share with siblings and, in a large family, some even had to sleep head to tail in order to pack more into a bed. Beds consisted of sheets and blankets and needed to be made up daily. Duvets were uncommon and viewed as the curious invention of foreigners. Bedrooms were not generally heated. Sometimes when my mother came in to wake me up in winter, she would say that Jack Frost had come in the night to paint the windows and I found the condensation on the panes frosted over with delightful patterns – a joy missed in a centrally heated home. Nevertheless, main bedrooms often had a fireplace so that if necessary – perhaps during illness or unduly cold weather – a coal fire could be lit. Electric blankets had not been invented, but if you could afford it, a hot-water bottle warmed at least part of the bed.

As sheets and blankets were tucked under the mattress, a hot-water bottle, particularly the earthenware rather than rubber variety, often got moved to one side of the bed and dragged the bedclothes off. Should you not have been able to afford a proper hot-water bottle, a warmed brick or even a stone served the same purpose. Warming pans had generally gone out of fashion.

Water bottles were not without their problems; on more than one occasion I found in the morning that I had a blister on my leg caused by the heat, while at other times I would wake up with a wet bed caused by a leaking seal, or perished rubber, unless it had been caused by another problem. Some people knitted woolly covers for their hot-water bottles, but I found that they prevented the spread of heat over the whole bed and preferred not to use them. Their surface was not so nice to the feel as rubber because it had a rough, rather than smooth, texture. Bed-socks were a mixed blessing because, although at first they kept your feet warm, I found the following morning that they had come off during the night.

Bedrooms generally contained a bed, wardrobe and set of drawers. If a house lacked a bathroom, or a family was large and the bathroom needed to be supplemented, a bedroom might have had a washstand: a table with a marble top on which stood a large basin and ewer containing water – cold, unless you had a maid who could

Girls' toy household equipment. (Hamley's 1937 catalogue)

bring you some hot. You were thus able to wash in your bedroom.

In that decade you did not have to be rich to afford a maid. Girls from large families would be pleased to leave their noisy, crowded home to live in a more spacious, quieter, pleasanter house for just their keep and a little pocket money. The work they were expected to do as cleaner, cook and nursemaid was often no more than they had to do at home and they were being paid to do it.

The majority of children didn't have a clock in their bedroom; it was unnecessary as their parents would wake them if they were not already up. Mum and Dad probably had an alarm clock that needed winding daily, ticked loudly and had intriguing luminous hands and numbers, while downstairs there was probably a clock in the living room and maybe the kitchen; but remember, money was short so you avoided spending it unnecessarily. Most clocks were of the clockwork variety and, unlike electric ones, failed from time to time. The better ones could be repaired at a price, but cheaper ones were thrown away and a replacement bought instead.

The bathroom, if you had one, contained a bath and hand basin. If hot and cold running water were available – and this was still a luxury in the thirties – the water might have been heated by the back-boiler fitted to the dining room fire; a boiler in the kitchen; or an electric or gas heater in the bathroom. Gas heaters were dangerous as they produced unpleasant fumes, had a bypass light which sometimes went out, filled the room with gas and always made a loud explosion when turned on to heat the water; they were therefore highly fascinating to small children.

Due to the difficulty of bathing – showers were practically unknown in the thirties – many people only had a bath weekly. The bathroom may have contained the dirty-linen basket, or it may have been kept on the landing. There was often a small cabinet in the bathroom for medicines and shaving equipment. For those living in

Scottish tenements without a bathroom, young children had a bath in front of the fire, but older children and adults used the corporation's public baths. If there was no bathroom and no public bath available, you bathed in a tin bath in front of the dining room fire, hot water being provided by the washday copper or a kettle.

Although safety razors were available, many men preferred the cut-throat razor which needed sharpening on a leather strap, sometimes cut from a railway carriage whose windows were raised and lowered by this means. In addition to sharpening his razor, a father's leather could also be used to punish a child.

Toilets: there were many varieties. Quite a few homes didn't have their own and so shared one, perhaps having to cross a yard to reach it. Others had a privy at the bottom of the garden with a bucket below the seat, the contents of which had to be disposed of periodically, although sometimes the seat might have been over a stream and whatever fell through the hole would be washed away.

One day, a boy, whose privy was beside a brook, was tempted to push the structure into the water. When his father had retrieved it and was questioning the boy to determine what had happened, the boy tentatively asked his father if he knew the story of George Washington. Hearing that he had, the boy confessed to the crime, but was given a good hiding. The lad pleaded, 'But Dad, George Washington's father didn't do that.' 'No,' replied his father, 'but George Washington's father wasn't sitting on that tree branch.'

Houses built in the thirties generally had a toilet on each floor, but older ones often had only one for the whole house. Whatever the case, it was common for a chamber pot to be found under a bed, the vessel often referred to as a 'guzunder' (goes under).

As strict economy had to be practised, many people did not use toilet paper but tore or cut newspaper into convenient-sized sheets, or used paper bags. If you were rather better off, you might have had a toilet roll for visitors' use in the upstairs lavatory. In practice, many people preferred to use newspaper as it was more absorbent and did the job better than the shiny paper used for the rolls.

Because many families only had just enough income for day-to-day requirements, the type of flooring varied. If you could afford it, you would choose carpet, if not for every room, then perhaps just for the lounge. The next best thing was linoleum, but the cheapest covering was floorcloth – really just a painted cloth. Lino or oil cloth was polished with Mansion, while some front doorsteps were given a red polish. As Mother was usually at home all day, she had time to keep the house looking spick and span.

A cheap and useful hobby was making rugs. Discarded fabric would be made into strips and tied into a canvas sack backing. A more upmarket family would use lengths of new coarse wool. These rugs could be made while listening to the radio or talking to friends.

A typical suburban house would have had a garden at the front with a lawn, flower bed and perhaps a fish

Here are the **HAMLEYS** the **DOLL'S ESTATE AGENTS** Tri-ang Dolls' Houses

The Modern Touch

No. 60 Doll's House
With half-timbered gables and metal framed windows which open. Tiled sun porch, steps and dummy shrubs. Two rooms fitted electric wall lights. Red tiled roof. 14″ wide.
PRICE 10/6
Carriage 1/-

No. 50 Doll's House
Ultra modern design with opening front. Two rooms fitted with electric wall lights, fireplaces and metal framed windows. Opening front door with staircase. Built in garage with opening doors. Finished in cream and green. 21″ wide.
PRICE 15/-
Carriage 1/6

No. 72 Doll's House
A full-sized house of fashionable Tudor design. Half-timbered gables at front. Built in garage with opening doors. Two bedrooms, dining room, bathroom and kitchen with range, dresser and sink. Staircase and landing. Front opens in four pieces. Side entrance with porch and seat. Metal framed windows which open and imitation green shutters. Fireplaces in all rooms, red tiled roof. Steps and dummy shrubs. Imitation flowered front. Four electric lights and switches. Width 47½″. Battery for lights, 6d. each.
PRICE 59/6

DOLL'S HOUSES
4th FLOOR

No. 62 Doll's House
Large double fronted model with four rooms and staircase Built in garage, opening metal framed windows, red tiled roof. Steps and dummy shrubs and nicely flowered front. Half timbered gables. Fitted four electric lights.
PRICE 22/6

No. 71 Doll's House
Popular design with half-timbered gables and large bay window. Tiled porch with seat and built in garage. Three rooms fitted electric wall lights. Opening metal framed windows with curtains. Front of house hinged to open. Grey tiled roof. Width 27″.
PRICE 39/6

Page 65

Dolls' houses imitating 1930s architecture. (Hamley's 1937 catalogue)

pond, while at the rear would be a small lawn and much larger vegetable plot for growing cabbage, root vegetables and celery, with perhaps a fruit tree and some soft fruit.

As well as underclothes, boys usually wore grey socks held up by garters, a grey or white shirt, grey trousers, a hand-knitted pullover and grey jacket. Up to about 13, they wore shorts rather than long trousers. Shorts or trousers were held up by either braces or a belt, the latter having a snake-shaped clip. Braces tended to be worn in the winter when they could be covered by a jacket, but a belt was favoured for the summer as it was considered 'not nice' to show braces. A cap, usually emblazoned with a school badge, would be worn out of doors, but taken off indoors or in church (it was rude to keep a hat on indoors), but left on in shops. Men and boys always covered their head with a cap, boater, trilby, bowler or Stetson when outdoors. A tie was always worn – lack of one indicated that you were too poor to afford one. Boys wore a school tie. Boys' raincoats, for wet or cold weather, were usually blue unless their school had chosen another colour.

If you wore shoes, they were generally black. Some favoured boots, which were warmer in winter and offered more ankle support, but all the lacing required was a problem if you were required to change quickly before and after sport or physical education. Some very poor children ran about barefoot, which, although it seems barbarous today, was not an entirely bad thing as their feet did not run the risk of being deformed by ill-fitting footwear, and the soles of their feet grew hard and thus were not made uncomfortable by stones. Some children whose parents could afford footwear actually preferred to go about barefoot.

Unless you were very poor, most men and boys had two suits, one for everyday use and another for Sundays. If you wished to appear smart, you would have a handkerchief protruding from the top pocket of your jacket and wear a flower in your buttonhole. Men's shirt collars were detachable and although a collar might have been washed daily, the shirt was probably only washed weekly. Cuffs were held together by links rather than buttons. In the thirties, rather than wear a suit to a sporting event, many older lads and men were able to afford a sports jacket. Even on the beach, unless it was particularly hot, many men wore jackets, waistcoats and ties, while their swimming costumes generally covered their chests as well as their lower parts. Similarly, women's and girls' costumes were very modest. Ties were kept straight by a tiepin which may have been expensive and bejewelled or an inexpensive one, bought at Woolworths. Men's socks were held in place by suspenders.

Schoolgirls wore black or brown shoes or sandals, a dress, a gymslip and woolly cardigan, and at other times dressed similarly to women with a blouse and skirt, although those who were daring in the late thirties wore trousers and headscarves.

Due to the shortage of money, men's and children's fashions varied little, but women's fashions were very wide ranging, partly because they could make their own or modify existing garments.

Some women and older girls made their own dresses from paper patterns, either purchased or given away in women's magazines.

When clothes and socks became worn or damaged, they were generally repaired by the women and girls of the household, while shoes were taken to the cobbler's, although if you were handy, you might be able to nail on a new heel, or stick on a new sole. At home we had what was known as a 'last' and this was valuable for replacing a heel, or hammering nails into the leather to prevent it wearing out. Nails with special heads could be bought for this purpose.

Knitting was very popular and helped provide stylish clothes which were warm and only cost the price of the wool, or nothing at all if you unravelled an old garment. Most women knitted cardigans, jumpers, swimsuits and socks. The advantage of knitting was that it could be done almost anytime and anywhere, when talking to a friend, for example, or listening to the radio, or travelling on a bus, tram or train. Many children wore at least one garment knitted by their mother.

Both girls and boys enjoyed French knitting, often producing a long chain which could be wound into a circle to make a useful mat on which a cake or plate of biscuits could be displayed. Sometimes friends exchanged wool which meant a pleasing variety so you weren't looking at the same colour all the time.

One custom, which was dying out in the thirties, was that some poor children were sewn into their clothes in the winter until the following spring, by which time they were, to say the least, somewhat odorous.

To save money, rather than pay a barber, a parent could cut a child's hair using a pudding basin to keep the edges level. To keep their hair neat and tidy, men and boys smeared Brylcreem, or some similar substance, to smooth it down and retain it in the correct position. Girls usually had their hair cut by their mothers.

When a tooth came out, I always placed it in my slipper before going to bed and during the night the tooth fairy collected it (I don't know what use it was to them) and left a threepenny bit in exchange. One evening I thought it would be exciting to write a letter to this fairy to see if I received a reply. The next morning, I was thrilled to find I had a letter from Fairy Forget-Me-Not, whose handwriting, I observed, was very similar to my mother's.

During the day, when the family was up and about, it was general practice for back doors to be left unlocked. It was really quite safe; neighbours would spot a stranger, and neighbours didn't steal from each other. Any burglar would have come from further afield and that would have meant by foot, cycle or public transport, none of which would have been ideal for a quick getaway. A thief would not have been rich enough to have had a car, nor even known how to drive.

The increased use of cars since the thirties has brought about two serious declines in our country. Firstly, thieves can make a quick getaway to another part of the country and, secondly, we jump into our cars and drive off without speaking to our neighbours. In the thirties, we would have spoken to them when walking to the bus or tram stop, or when cycling past them.

About once a year, a tramp, I don't know if it was the same one, appeared at the back door with a tin can and asked my mother if she would kindly fill it with tea. She always kindly obliged. They were different times.

Coal delivery was an education. Our coal cellar had a very low ceiling and was under the dining room. Several times a year, the extremely clean Fordson lorry stopped outside our gate and the two coalmen, each dressed in a sleeveless leather jacket, brought in the hundredweight (112lb) sacks of coal.

My parents never swore, so some words were not in my vocabulary. Stooping low as the coalmen brought the sacks into the cellar, I would hear a thump as a head hit the ceiling followed by some very naughty words. Then the coalmen would bring in some more sacks, I'd hear another thump and, 'B****y hell, I've done it again!' They never seemed to learn from their experience.

Another delivery to the cellar was coke from the gas works, but as this was stored in the part of the cellar with a higher ceiling, its arrival was not so instructive. The coke was used for the boiler in the kitchen, which provided hot water for the bathroom and kitchen.

Gas lighting was becoming outdated by this time, but was still very prevalent in older houses and had the benefit – except on a hot summer's evening – of providing heat as well as light. These lights had to be lit very carefully or the match would break the delicate mantle and that would mean the expense of buying a new one. Gas lighting also created a smell; as soon as you entered the front door, you could tell if a house was lit by gas.

In the thirties, babies were exposed to much more fresh air than they are today. A mother fortunate enough to have a garden wrapped her baby up warmly and left it outside in the pram where it was quite safe and could absorb the sights, sounds and smells of the natural world.

Mealtimes for young children were much the same as today: food was served in an oval high-sided plate so it could not be pushed off the edges and was fairly difficult to overturn. Food was eaten with a silver spoon which had a large curly handle so that the implement could not easily be swallowed. The food was propelled on to the spoon by what was known as a pusher – a small rectangle attached to a handle at 90 degrees. I remember that one day I had to manage without mine. An aunt had told my mother that her daughter had swallowed hers to her detriment.

Turning now to the subject of writing – if you were scribbling a quick note, you might well have used a pencil, but for anything more formal, a pen and ink would have been used. This would have been a dip pen and bottle of ink, but a really modern person would have used a fountain pen with a lever to draw ink from the bottle. You could write many words before a fountain pen needed refilling, but a dip pen would only last for about one line of writing. Another alternative was a propelling pencil which didn't need sharpening as the lead could be extended. Most homes did not own a typewriter.

It was all too easy to spill a bottle of ink and make a dreadful mess. I was given an unspillable ink bottle. Made of glass, its sides curved inwards and downwards so that when tipped, the ink was retained by these sides and did not run out. Unfortunately, I did not fully appreciate exactly how it functioned. Once, when a cousin paid me a visit, I made a violent thrust towards him with this ink bottle claiming, 'It's unspillable!' And so it was if it were tipped gently, but as I'd jerked it towards him, a splash of ink flew out through the space where I dipped my pen and rather spoilt the appearance of his new suit. Despite the efforts of my embarrassed mother, his suit was never really the same again.

It was always exciting to see the postman approach the house. It was more than likely that he was delivering something for your parents but there was always just a small chance that a kind relation had sent a present, or a friend a postcard.

There were two posts daily: one in the morning and a second post later. This meant that if you put a letter addressed to someone in the same town in the postbox early in the day, it would be delivered with the second post. It was an extremely useful way to communicate quickly in the days when most households hadn't a telephone. Most of those who did have one used it mainly for business purposes. During the week before Christmas, the post would be delivered about four times a day – this was before the era of posting Christmas cards very early; in fact, the postman even delivered on Christmas Day itself.

For the many who didn't possess a telephone, sending a telegram was a quick means of relaying a message if you couldn't deliver it personally. Telegrams could be sent from any post office and were delivered by lads on red push bikes. I remember receiving one when church choir practice had to be cancelled suddenly because of deep snow.

As many people had both a daily morning and evening paper because free papers were then unknown, this offered two chances of securing a paper round with its financial benefits.

It was rare to spot aircraft, but sometimes when one appeared, it might have been 'looping the loop' or writing a word using a vapour trail. I can remember one morning rushing indoors from the garden shouting, 'Mummy, Mummy, I've seen a plane and it's writing "Persil" in the sky!'

As there was no National Health Service at that time, medical attention normally came at a price, although there were societies that you could join which, for a monthly fee, entitled you to be seen by a doctor and receive medication. Some hospitals were free, but others had to be paid for, and furthermore, not everyone could afford the services of a dentist or optician. Many homes owned a book such as *The Universal Home Doctor* which helped you to self-diagnose and decide whether a few days in bed would put you right or whether you should pay for a doctor, either to come and see you at home (more expensive), or go to see them in the surgery (cheaper). If the latter, you may well have had to wait in a room for an hour or more as there was no appointment system and, even if there had been one, few could have used it because most households didn't have a telephone to make the appointment in the first place.

Carnivals and processions were always of interest to the young and offered opportunities for new experiences. The British Legion Fete was popular and I can remember seeing someone dive from a high platform into a tank of burning liquid. On another occasion, my father took me out one evening to a nearby main road where we waited and, in due course, a procession of decorated vehicles came along advertising a variety of products, some of them designed as large bottles or whatever object the vehicle was advertising – exciting because they were unusual.

Women tended not to go out to work unless they were single or had a disabled husband. Those who did were usually teachers, nurses, shop assistants or receptionists, or helped their husbands. There were obvious advantages to not working as it meant mothers were able to spend more time looking after their children, especially if they were ill at home. They had time to cook meals for the family, a much cheaper option than dining out or having meals delivered – a service not available at that time. Money could be saved by making and mending clothes, knitting, sewing and doing embroidery.

Shops were open Mondays to Fridays and also Saturday mornings, closing on Saturdays at about 1 p.m. As shop assistants had to work Saturday mornings, a day – usually a Wednesday or Thursday – was deemed 'early closing day' so that shop workers could have an afternoon off. It was a legal measure and only repealed in 1994. Shops closed on bank holidays, and thus if Christmas Day fell on a Monday, it meant that, as shops were always closed on Sundays, the last day to shop before Christmas Day would have been Saturday and then the shops would not have re-opened until the following Wednesday. This caused quite a problem in pre-refrigeration times. Greengrocers wouldn't have had fresh vegetables because none would have been picked from the Sunday to the Tuesday.

Another feature of the decade was 'market day'. Most towns and even large villages had a weekly market where cattle were bought and sold. Farmers attended to discover the latest prices and brought their wives with them to sell eggs, butter, cheese and cream. As more people travelled by train on market day than any other, often a branch-line train would be strengthened by an extra coach or two that day.

Some families were highly concerned about the job security of the wage earner. If you were the shop manager of a nationwide company selling suits, for example, head office may have expected you to sell a certain number of suits weekly and, if the number fell below the quota, then it was the sack for you. It was not unknown to see a manager in tears outside his shop late on a Saturday pleading for custom. Hardly the 'good old days'.

Butchers had sawdust on the floor to soak up any blood from the meat around, with sides of beef hanging up, while pigs' heads on the counter looked gruesome. Rabbits, hares and poultry could also be seen hanging up, tempting customers to buy. Fishmongers had an open window with a sloping slab beyond it on which fish were attractively displayed.

Some homes displayed a bowl of water with floating plastic swans. Camphor was placed on the ends of the swans and the gas coming off when it touched the water propelled the swans across the bowl at a suitably dignified speed.

In terms of first aid, iodine was usually kept in the house and initially used as an antiseptic, but later, Dettol or TCP was the favoured product. Cuts were protected by a bandage rather than a plaster.

My mother did not have much faith in my teacher's first-aid skills. When I fell down in the playground and cut my knee, I went to the teacher on duty and she washed it and put some nice-smelling ointment on the wound and covered it with a bandage. Needlessly I thought, when I told my mother what had happened, she unwrapped it, washed it again, but failed to put any sweet-smelling ointment on before she bandaged it up again.

A common drug found in the medicine cupboard at this time was ipecacuanha and, if the doctor was called, I dreaded him telling my mother that she should give me a spoonful of it. Ipecacuanha is the dried root of a South American shrub and it is a powerful emetic. I expect my mother dreaded it, too, because when I was sick over the sheets it meant that she had to change them and have them laundered.

Other staples found in the medicine cupboard were aspirin, stomach powder, Milk of Magnesia, Beecham's Powders (good for colds/flu) and cough mixture.

Diphtheria was a prevalent killer – in fact, I nearly died of it myself. Almost all children caught chickenpox, German measles, measles, mumps, tonsillitis and whooping cough, and there was the dread of catching polio, a life-threatening disease which killed or crippled thousands and required them to have to use corrective shoes, crutches or leg callipers. Tuberculosis was another killer that 1930s families had to face.

One thing we did get in the thirties which we don't receive now is free samples through the letter box. Sometimes it was breakfast cereals or a simple, but often useful, gadget such as a needle threader from Kleeneze or Betterware; at other times it was a card cut-out toy.

The police officer on his beat was a familiar sight in both town and country. They kept an eye open for trouble, testing doors at night, looking for objects out of place or unusual goings-on. They took pride in keeping their beats crime free. In town they would walk, but in the country, they cycled as they had a larger area to cover, probably several villages. Children respected them and were taught to speak to them if in trouble and, unlike today, police officers were easy to find. Police telephone stands were introduced in the thirties. Red in colour, they had a blue light at the top which flashed if a message needed to be conveyed to a police officer on the beat. These telephones could also be used by the public for emergency calls to the police, fire or ambulance services. Should a police officer need help from colleagues, he could also summon them by blowing his Acme whistle: one long blast followed by three short ones.

Periodically, the gas company or electricity supplier would send a man to read the meters. From time to time the gas supply would falter and the company would have to come and blow the pipe to get rid of water. They then let this trickle down the path outside the house and it smelled revolting. We do not experience this with North Sea gas nowadays. There was no water meter then as water consumption was covered by the house rates. A water company official would nevertheless pay a visit to listen at the stopcock on the pavement outside the house to determine whether any water was running away.

Two

GAMES AND HOBBIES

How much pocket money a child received varied according to a father's wealth; some children were not given anything, but the average was a penny a week. This could be supplemented by performing jobs such as mowing the lawn or running errands (called 'messages' in Scotland). There was the possibility of earning money from a paper round or making deliveries for tradespeople, but 'better class' children, particularly those attending grammar school, were not expected to do a paper round but instead use their time and energy for studying.

Younger children played with wooden bricks, lead farm animals and Noah's Arks, and also invented imaginative games, pretending to run shops 'selling' such items as old tins, bottles and pieces of coloured glass, perhaps using buttons as money. Playing 'mothers and fathers' was another highly popular game and girls often did the real thing anyway by helping Mother

The author in his pedal Vauxhall car, 1936. (G.T. Maggs)

cook, clean the silver, and sweep and dust the house. If their parents could afford one, a pedal car or tricycle provided hours of fun and exercise, as did the rather cheaper scooter. Children of the thirties spent much more time out of doors than children do today.

Before having a bicycle, many children learnt to balance on a scooter, one leg standing on its platform while the other provided the propulsive power. Although scooters were not usually fitted with a brake, this posed no problem as a heel could be pressed down on the rear wheel to stop the forward motion. Quite a number of scooters in use were made by fathers who were skilful with their hands.

Children's games were mostly unorganised and, due to the shortage of money, they generally didn't cost anything. Hobbies often centred around a type of collection. With less attention in those days being given to preserving endangered species, birds' eggs and butterflies were collected – finding and identifying them being part of the fun. Bus, tram and railway tickets could be collected; bus tickets were usually different colours to denote different prices. Some were categorised geographically and had the names of fare stages printed on them. The conductor would punch the stage where the passenger boarded.

Railway tickets were colour-coded, with white denoting first class and green third class. They were pre-printed with the station of origin and destination on them. In addition, different tickets were available for different types of passengers: members of the armed forces, cheap day returns, half-day returns, workmen, etc. There was an almost infinite variety available.

As stations and trains were a familiar sight, you could collect engine numbers as a hobby and see how many different ones you could identify. Although the pastime was taken up by many children, it was only the Great Western Railway (GWR) that encouraged it, and it did so by publishing a book with the numbers arranged in different classes. For other railway companies, this information was almost impossible to obtain, and thus you didn't know how many numbers of a certain class of locomotive you still needed to get before you had a full set.

Station platforms were places where you could find exciting penny-in-the-slot machines. Such a spectacle was gripping because automated machines were far fewer in those days. You put your penny in the slot and pulled out a drawer to retrieve a thin bar of chocolate or packet of chewing gum. If the drawer failed to open, a good kick often did the trick. Then there were weighing

Colourful railway, tram and bus tickets were fun to collect. (Author's collection)

scales, but how many children wanted to know how much they weighed? Far more exciting was the machine that printed a label on an aluminium strip. It had a dial like a clock, but with letters instead of numbers. You inserted your penny and turned the pointer to the first letter of the word you required and pulled a handle towards you; this activated, punching the letter on to the aluminium strip. You then turned the pointer to the next letter, and so on. When you had finished punching your word, you pulled another lever and the strip emerged with your word, or words, on it. In all likelihood, the first time a child used this device was to produce a label bearing their own name.

Somewhat akin to collecting engine numbers was collecting vehicle registration index marks and, for many places, the two letters and four figures which identified the number of cars registered by that authority lasted for all, or certainly most, of the decade. When the allocation of letters and numbers reached 9999, the registration authorities added an A as a prefix to its letters. The letters, for example, OA Birmingham, became AOA, then BOA, and so on. In order to keep the registration plates the same size, three letters were followed by a maximum of three figures, and thus, when 999 was reached, a new prefix letter had to be introduced.

This system meant that new series appeared regularly and children had a much greater chance of seeing a plate with the figure '1', whereas in the earlier four-figure series '1' would have designated a very old car, either no longer in existence or only used on rare occasions. And so a new game was invented: look out for a '1', then try to find a '2', and so on.

Although very few new postal stamps appeared in the thirties – English commemoratives were rare – foreign stamps could be begged from friends and relatives. The decade had three kings: George V, Edward VIII and George VI, which meant stamps had to have a change of design for each new monarch, as well as one to commemorate the Silver Jubilee of George V. Children enjoyed consulting a Stanley Gibbons catalogue to discover the worth of their own stamp collection.

Smoking was popular in the thirties. As the cigarette packets were quite flimsy, the manufacturers inserted cards inside to reinforce them. The manufacturers produced exciting series to appeal to boys and included railways, footballers, flags, flowers, birds, etc., and also produced an attractive album, priced at 1*d*, with a special place for each of the fifty cards in a set. Boys were anxious to have a complete set and so pestered friends and relations to buy a certain brand of cigarette in order to acquire a missing card. They were also able to complete a set by swapping with friends. Some of the excitement of collecting cigarette cards, stamps and tickets was for their colour because most printing at that time was in black and white.

Periodically, marbles came into season. These very attractive, multicoloured glass balls could be used in several ways. The simplest was to put a marble down and challenge a friend to hit it with one of theirs from a certain distance. If they succeeded, they claimed your marble; if they missed, you took theirs.

Another form of entertainment using marbles was having a length of wood or strong card which you held vertically. Arches were cut at its base, the width of which was fractionally wider than a marble. Each arch was numbered, indicating just how many marbles your opponent would win from you if they managed to successfully propel their marble through the arches. If they failed, that marble was yours. As there was more chance of propelling a marble through a more central hole, the lowest numbers were in the middle and the highest were at each end.

Autumn was the season for conkers. It was fun finding the horse chestnuts, perhaps having to break open the spiked cases to see the glorious coloured and textured fruit inside. You borrowed a skewer from your mother – with or without her permission – punctured a hole all the way through the chestnut, threaded a string through the hole and tied a substantial knot in it to prevent the chestnut flying off. You then challenged your friend to a conker fight, taking it in turns to hit the other's nut. The one who destroyed the other's was the winner, their conker becoming a 'one-er'. Should your conker have survived a second battle, it became a 'two-er', and so on. The winning conker owner inherited the score of the defeated conker owner, and thus, if your 'three-er' beat a 'two-er', it meant that, in addition to yours becoming a 'four-er', you added the 'two-er' to make it a 'six-er'.

Conkers. (Stanze from Germany, Baden-Württemberg, CC SA 2.0 via WikemediaCommons)

Playing conkers was not for the faint-hearted as it was all too easy for a conker to strike a knuckle or head quite painfully. Needless to say, when the health & safety era came along, it was banned by many head teachers – who had played and enjoyed it themselves in their youth!

Cricket and football were always popular and, if a field or park was not to hand, there was always the street, which probably saw very little traffic. Danger came from the risk of breaking windows or being shouted at by neighbours who wanted a quiet nap and disliked having a noisy game outside their house.

Some boys liked to feel they wielded power and a bow and arrow were very easy weapons to make – just a flexible branch and some string for the bow, and another length of wood for the arrow. Depending on its construction, a bow could either be fairly harmless or very lethal, as could a catapult. The one I had was made from thinnish wire and not very strong elastic, and was probably not strong enough to kill even a bird, but one made from the inner tube of a car could prove fatal to both people and animals.

I owned a dart board and, when it started to disintegrate, I was surprised to discover that it consisted of a long roll of paper, probably something like an eighth of a mile in length.

Cycling grew in popularity in the thirties as by this time most roads and lanes had been tarred and had a reasonable surface. A cycle, once purchased, gave you the freedom to travel far and wide at virtually no expense, over a much larger area than one could walk. It was more fun cycling in the company of others, so cycling clubs proliferated, some covering trips of more than 100 miles a day. It was easier if you shared the effort of turning the pedals with someone else and so tandems became popular and were produced in three varieties: one for men and boys, another for women and girls, and another for both genders.

This form of cycling leads me to a joke:

> Mother to Neighbour: My two lads have gone off cycling when I distinctly told them not to.
> Neighbour: Tandem?
> Mother: No, not yet, but just wait till they get back!

Early cycles were fitted with fixed gears, but in line with the slightly improved standard of living in the thirties, some cyclists were able to afford a Sturmey-Archer 3-speed gear, or the derailleur type, which literally derailed the chain from one sprocket wheel to another. Drop handle-bars were another so-called improvement which was introduced at this time, the advantage of which was that – if you were game – you could race along at top speed. Alternatively, you could choose to cycle more slowly and calmly absorb the beauty of your surroundings.

For those who enjoyed organised activities, Scouts, Guides, Cubs and Brownies became very popular, while for the less active, the public library would be a haven of peace in which to select books to borrow, read newspapers and magazines, or carry out research.

Boys – and in the thirties it was generally only boys – might have joined a church choir. You were given a uniform: cassock, surplice and ruff or collar, which thus made you feel superior to those who just wore ordinary clothes, and you received payment each quarter. It also meant that in a choir you were as important as an adult and where else would this be the case? As a chorister, although you probably didn't realise it at the time, you also received useful musical training and, if you listened to the sermons, you learnt how to become a good citizen.

The thirties was the decade when the radio became an important part of many homes. It was called a 'wireless' as, unlike the telephone, it brought sound to your house without needing a wire. In 1930, comparatively few homes had one, yet by 1939, almost all homes did. The BBC in those days was very prim and proper; presenters wore evening dress even though they couldn't be seen by their listeners. Children were highly delighted on one occasion when they heard one confused presenter announcing, 'The next piece of music will be "The bum of the flightle bee".'

Youngsters enjoyed *Children's Hour*, the main presenter being Derek McCulloch (Uncle Mac), who was assisted in different regions by various aunties. The stories, music and plays were all very entertaining. Sadly, when war was declared in 1939, *Children's Hour* was shortened from its traditional hour to forty minutes, but still retained its then rather meaningless title. *Children's Hour* was broadcast from 1922 until

1964 and I had just got my foot in the door as a speaker and made several broadcasts on the programme when it was withdrawn due to the fact that most children had started to watch television.

Sandy MacPherson and Reginald Foort were popular broadcasters who also played cinema organs which had originally been installed during the silent film era. In the thirties, however, they were used for entertainment between films. Another musical offering was given by Henry Hall's Band. Listening to his signature tune as he signed off at the end of the programme was the signal for my bedtime. Bands were highly popular, some being amateur such as those from Grimethorpe Colliery, Black Dyke Mills and Foden Motor Works.

The series of thrillers featuring the amateur detective Paul Temple was broadcast between 1938 and 1968 and was based on the novels of Francis Durbridge and had as its signature tune 'Coronation Scot'. I remember the coffin of one of my railway enthusiast friends being carried out of the church with the organ playing this melody; the coffin bore the warning, 'Beware of the Trains'.

A popular programme on Saturday evenings was *In Town Tonight* in which a police officer 'stopped the traffic' so that interesting people could be interviewed. At the end of the programme, the police officer declared, 'Carry on London.' Some elderly listeners actually believed that the traffic really was halted for the duration of the programme.

Most of the early wireless sets were powered either by batteries or accumulators. A new battery had to be bought when the old one went flat, but an accumulator could be taken to a garage or tramway depot to be recharged, this proving cheaper than the price of a new battery. By 1939, many homes had mains electricity so, by that time, batteries and accumulator sets were becoming old fashioned.

To obtain good reception, a long aerial was required – quite often stretching from the house to the far end of the garden (assuming you had one). As a wireless was relatively expensive to buy, some people hired one, but although this avoided the initial cost outlay, in the long run it proved more expensive. Being so costly, most homes only had one radio and this formed the centrepiece of the living room; the whole family gathered around to listen to the news, comedy, drama, concert or talk. As there was no means of recording a broadcast at home, you had to listen to it live, or miss it forever, but for those who could afford it, there was a sister publication to the *Radio Times* titled *The Listener* which reprinted some of the more important items.

History was made when at 3 p.m. on Christmas Day, 1932, King George V made his first broadcast to the empire from a box room at Sandringham, although contemporary newspaper photographs showed him in rather more luxurious surroundings. The transmission was technically difficult for the outside broadcast engineers as they had to reserve phone lines in advance.

Radio entertainers became almost like gods and their weekly shows were not to be missed. They often used catchphrases which invoked howls of laughter every time. Tommy Trinder, Arthur Askey and Richard (Stinker) Murdoch were such entertainers. The sisters Elsie and Doris Waters played Gert and Daisy in comic sketches and were greatly loved.

Another performer was George Formby who sang and played a ukulele. I remember being taught by a friend how to make up a story about him. You took a match box – very easy to find as people were always using matches to light cigarettes, pipes or the gas stove – a length of cotton and a shirt button. One end of the cotton was knotted and threaded through from the inside to the outside of the matchbox, making it into a sound box. The cotton was then threaded through a hole in the shirt button and the other end of the cotton held between finger and thumb, pulled taut. You then asked a friend to hold the matchbox to their ear.

You then said to your enraptured audience, 'One day, George Formby was on the stage playing his ukulele' – and as you spoke, you plucked the cotton to make a ukulele twang. You continued, 'Then suddenly he collapses and an ambulance is sent for. The ambulance driver starts the engine.' Here, you twanged the cotton and button to make an engine-starting noise. It could be made even more dramatic if it failed to start the first time. When you had managed to start it, you slid the button along the taut cotton to make the sound of the ambulance en route.

If you thought your audience had not become weary of listening, once George was on board the ambulance, you could re-start the engine and take him to hospital.

Another popular construction in the thirties was the transformation of an empty cotton reel, a Kirby hair clip, strong elastic band, a pencil or thin, short stick and a short length of candle into a tank; although a great deal of imagination was required to do it, it was tremendous fun to make and operate.

The Kirby grip went across the hole in the reel on one side to hold one end of the rubber band. Using a sharp knife – mind you didn't cut your fingers – you cut a slice of candle, about a quarter of an inch thick (we didn't use metric measurements in the thirties). You then gouged out the wick and made a hole large enough to push the rubber band through. The rubber band should then have passed through both the reel and the wax disc. To finish, you threaded the pencil (preferably a long one) through the other loop of the band. The pencil was then turned round and round, the band twisted – careful, not too much or it would break – and when you thought you'd wound it tight enough, you placed it on the floor and it would move. (You've probably worked out that the purpose of the wax was to prevent the band unravelling too quickly.) To get traction on the carpet, the edges of the wooden reel needed to be serrated using a pen knife or craft knife.

Another exciting construction to make was a boomerang, which actually worked! You needed a smallish piece of card, such as a post card or an old packet, and had to cut out a curved banana shape about 4 inches long. You'd place this on the edge of a book, about half of it overhanging, then, with a pencil, you gave it a sharp rap. It would fly off and then return to you – no, not actually back on to the book, but probably at your feet.

An easily produced piece of equipment providing hours of entertainment was a working telephone. You just needed two cocoa tins and a length of string; cocoa tins were better for the job than tins of beans as they didn't have serrated edges which could cut your ear. A hole was punched in the base of each tin, the string threaded through and secured by a knot. Pulling the string taut, you placed the open end of one tin against an ear, then your friend, some distance away, spoke into the open end of the other tin and – lo and behold – you could hear what was said.

A parachute was another easily made toy. You tied one end of four short lengths of string to each corner of your handkerchief, preferably clean and ironed. A toy airman or other figure was then secured to the other ends of the lengths of string. You opened your bedroom window and dropped it out. I found the game soon paled as it was difficult to introduce any variety, and running up and down stairs was tiring and did not always meet with the approval of the domestic authorities.

A boat could easily be made from half a walnut shell ballasted with hot candle wax to prevent it from turning turtle. Before the wax solidified, a cocktail stick or something similar was pushed in to form a mast which had been pushed through the centre of a square paper sail. These boats could be sailed in a bath, basin or bowl. We held exciting races with friends by blowing our boat to the finishing line to win.

A spinner was fun to make and use, entertaining to both boys and girls. You needed a metal disc, though you could make do with one of heavyweight cardboard. You drilled a hole each side of the centre and threaded a length of strong string through both holes before tying the ends of the string together. You should then have had a loop of string each side of the disc. Using its weight, you spun the disc so that it twisted the string on each side. With your fingers in the loops, you moved both hands apart so that as the string unwound it made the disc spin. Immediately before it had completely unwound, you relaxed the tension on the string by bringing your hands together so that the weight of the disc, acting like a fly-wheel, twisted the string again. You continued pulling your hands apart and putting them together again like playing a concertina – until boredom set in.

Whether you lived in town or in the countryside, 'hide and seek' was always a very exciting game to play because it gave you a chance to feel superior by outwitting your opponent – the one having to find you.

'Kingy' was another exciting game; although it was sometimes played by girls as well, it was best suited to boys. You would throw a small soft ball, perhaps made from an old sock, at your friends. They could only defend themselves by punching the ball away. Should any other part of the body be hit by the ball, that person was 'out' and had to join the attacking group; the winner was the last one out.

Fishing in ponds, lakes, rivers, canals or even the sea was a cheap pastime, with the added benefit of catching something free to eat if you were lucky. It did not appeal to everyone because it required patience. My father was keen on fishing and had hoped to get me interested. On the first occasion, sitting on the river bank, I quickly became bored when nothing was caught in the first five minutes. To some, however, the expectation and anticipation was all part of the fun and could be compared to collecting locomotive numbers: you never knew what would come along, it may be a rare engine or a more familiar one, or, indeed, a large fish or a small one. A bonus to fishing or collecting engine numbers in a rural location was that you could observe wildlife, both flora and fauna, in those quiet moments.

'Pass the peas' was an exciting challenge. You were given a straw and two dishes, one empty and one containing a certain number of dried peas. On being given the 'off', you had to transfer the peas from one dish to the other by sucking your straw to see who could do it the quickest to win.

An equally challenging game could be played with milk bottles. A clothes peg was tied to one end of a length of string, the other end being tied to the loop or

belt at the back of your trousers. You placed a milk bottle
on the floor just behind your open legs and then, without using your hands, tried to drop the clothes peg and
string into the bottle before anyone else did.

Swimming was a good, healthy activity whether in
the municipal baths or outdoors in rivers, canals, lakes or
the sea. Many children learnt to swim on their first visit
to the baths by literally being thrown in at the deep end.
Money being short, the swimming costume was usually
a knitted affair made by Mum or your big sister, and in
the early thirties, men had their chests covered as well
as their lower parts. Knitted costumes quickly became
soggy and droopy and looked cumbersome, and consequently it was hard to glide through the water.

The thirties were the time when go-ahead local
authorities built lidos either in park-like surroundings
or on bathing beaches. Lifeguards were rarely on duty
in those days and that nearly cost my friend his life. One
afternoon, a neighbour drove him to a lido. There, my
friend enjoyed watching people dive from a high board
and then he moved to the other end of the pool where
there was a slide. Although usually nervous of water, he
thought that he'd imitate the others and slide down into
the pool. He lay at the bottom of the pool, in about
1½ feet of water, unable to stand up due to the slippery pool floor where his feet could find no purchase.
He thought he was going to drown, but fortunately, the
neighbour who had brought him spotted his problem
and picked him up.

'Kick the can' was a game favoured by Scottish lads during the long, dark evenings. A tin was placed on a manhole cover and you kicked it as far as you could. You nominated someone to be 'it' (the one designated to collect it), while the rest of the players were required to hide. Once 'it' had retrieved the can, it was then banged down on the manhole cover as a signal to the others that they were starting to search for them. When you were discovered, you became a prisoner and were out of the game, but if someone free was able to kick the can, that released you. The game finished when 'it' could not find any more.

The person to be 'it' was chosen by getting into a circle and dipping – that is chanting a rhyme such as 'Eeny, meeny, miny, moe', and pointing to another in turn; the last one left became 'it'. Another way was if someone came along and asked if they could join the game you'd say, 'Yes, you're "it"'!'

Dundee boys enjoyed 'Keepie uppie' which involved heading a ball continuously against the wall of a tenement. Another, more profitable, activity was collecting horse manure off the streets and selling it for garden fertiliser. A more vicious activity was pushing canes into a flower border, fixing a slightly opened matchbox on top to collect earwigs and then when they were trapped, having fun destroying them.

In addition to shop-bought skipping ropes, which were generally just for one person to use, if you had a long rope, several children could skip together, often chanting a rhyme such as:

Jelly on the plate; jelly on the plate;
Wiggle waggle, wiggle waggle,
Jelly on the plate.

A highly exhilarating, although rather dangerous, game was 'British bulldogs'. Two opposite sides of the play area were deemed to be 'safe' ground. One or two players, designated bulldogs, positioned themselves in the centre.

A bulldog then called out the name of one of the other players who was then required to run from one side to the other without being caught by a bulldog. If caught, however, and the captive could be held long enough for the bulldog to shout 'British bulldog: one, two, three', the runner became a bulldog. When the first runner had been caught, or safely reached the other side, all the other players had to try to cross without being captured. The game continued until all had become bulldogs, the winner being the last one caught.

'Touch', or 'tig' in some parts of the country, was popular, and also the more exciting 'Release touch' where someone guarded those touched by the 'he' and those who remained free could try to release them by touching them while trying to avoid being touched themselves. Although this was more exciting than the more basic touch, you needed more players to make it work properly. Another variety was 'Off-ground touch', where you could avoid being touched by getting above ground level such as on a bar or wall.

Cartwheels seemed mostly to have been performed by girls, although boys enjoyed watching this skilful gymnastic technique because it was always possible that the girls' knickers might be revealed. To perform a cartwheel, you stood up straight and, with great courage, threw yourself on to an outstretched arm and hopefully turned 360 degrees, touching the ground with the other hand, then one leg and then the other, until you were standing up straight again. Other games typically played by girls included counting the number of skips they could make until the rope became tangled; they were always trying to beat their previous best record.

'Hopscotch' was an energetic game played with a framework marked out in chalk on a path or quiet road. 'Leap-frog' offered good exercise. You stood in line with your friends and one of you bent over to allow the next in line to jump over your back; then they bent down in front of you, so that the third leap-frogger could vault over you both. When all of you were bent over, the first leap-frogger stood up and vaulted over all of you again.

'Knock Up Ginger' was great fun to play, although very unkind to the players' victims, especially elderly folk who found movement difficult. It could only be played in a street where two front doors were side by side and had door knockers – which was generally the case because electric doorbells were almost unknown in the thirties as knockers were cheaper. You tied two adjacent knockers together, knocked one and ran away. The occupant would open the door which made the string taut and lifted the knocker of the house next door. Not seeing anyone after opening the door, the householder would close it again which slackened the string and knocked next door's knocker and, when the occupant opened it, that would knock the knocker of the first house; the farce continued until the neighbours realised what was happening.

This game was best played after dark, especially as the street lights were relatively ineffective; you could easily hide and watch the outcome without being identified and your parents informed. A simpler form of the game was just knocking the knocker and then running away.

For less athletic children, there was 'Five stones', played with five small stones and one bigger one. You started by placing a small stone on the back of a hand and tossing it into the air, picking up the larger stone and catching the smaller one – all at the same time. This was repeated with two small stones on the back of the hand and continued until all five had been picked up. Your turn ended if you failed to catch any of the stones or failed to pick up the bigger one.

Another calm pastime was 'Cat's cradle': two children, usually girls, would wind a loop of string around their fingers to create patterns, including what was supposed to look like a cat's cradle. Another rather sedentary pastime was playing with a yo-yo. Although invented centuries earlier, it was not until the thirties that they could be manufactured cheaply. It consisted of a pair of joined discs with a deep groove between them in which a string was attached and wound. By means of its weight and momentum, it could be made to go up and down as it unwound and rewound.

A more challenging game for children with a literary frame of mind was making lists. You would see who could make the longest list of such subjects as birds, animals, fruits, trees or flowers.

A rather dull game which could be played by anyone was 'We all pat the dog', in which one person started off patting another and singing: 'We all pat the dog, we all pat the dog; heigh-ho, heigh-ho, we all pat the dog.' Usually, everyone around joined in and there could be twenty or so children patting one child.

Once, when I was a young lad and started singing the song and patting a child, I was surprised and horrified that he started to weep – there was no pain involved so perhaps it was just the fact of having a crowd round him, very nearly the whole school, that made him cry.

Iron hoops propelled and guided by a hooked stick provided simple entertainment, especially given that traffic was light and it was therefore safe to bowl it along the road and have exciting hoop races. In Scotland, the hoop was known as a 'cleat' and the hooked stick a 'girdu'.

Tops were enjoyed by everyone. A thin cord was wrapped around a large top which was then dropped to start the top spinning, the objective being to see whether you could keep it spinning longer than the others. Smaller tops had grooves around which the string was wrapped. It was then flung like a whip, causing the top to spin and fly through the air. The competition was to see how far you could throw a spinning top.

Most boys had one or more Dinky Toys, which provided hours of entertainment. They were exact replica models of real vehicles and could be purchased for several weeks' pocket money and pushed along the floor, a wall on the way to school, or over the eiderdown if you were ill in bed.

There were also Minics, similar in size and price but they included a clockwork motor. They weren't quite as popular as Dinky Toys as their use was restricted to a flat, level surface and were certainly no use in bed.

Poorer children had to make do with wooden toys made by their father, uncle or grandfather. Home-made ships, planes, locomotives, road vehicles and dolls' houses could provide hours of entertainment and really were just as good as shop-bought items. In fact, if personalised, they could even be better. Perhaps you had a model of the express locomotive that your grandfather drove that actually bore its correct number.

The joy of model railways was usually only for the middle class because a decent locomotive cost almost half the average weekly wage. Also, a model railway needed space, a minimum area of approximately 4ft by 6ft and, in some homes, this was just not available.

Models made by Hornby were the cheapest and gave good service, but more wealthy parents purchased those made by Bassett-Lowke, which were rather more lifelike and less like toys. Some very enterprising lads made a baseboard and created a town for their models, but most were content to use their imagination to make the floor covering become roads, fields or whatever suited their purpose at the time.

Until the mid-thirties, the smallest commercially made model railways were built to Gauge O, but then Trix Twin arrived on the scene and these were built half-size and deemed to be OO gauge. These were ideal as they would fit on a table top and were almost invariably electrically powered, whereas those with larger gauges were usually clockwork because they were cheaper. Messrs Hornby saw the possibilities and started producing OO gauge and called their models 'Dublo'. It was not realised at the time, but this was the gauge of the future and in the post-war period, almost all model railways were OO gauge – Gauge O became specialised.

One very exciting German toy I had was an *autobahn* in the shape of a figure of eight. A clockwork bus and racing car were also provided. With a friend operating one vehicle and I another, we imagined a criminal was on the bus and the racing car, full of police officers, had to intercept it. It was really the forerunner of Scalextric of the 1950s.

A German firm Schuco made excellent models with much play value. They produced a car which could be remotely steered by wire, another with a real gear lever and yet another which had an opening bonnet and which reversed automatically and – this seemed incredible – obeyed spoken orders. (The secret was a delicate membrane in the roof and when you said, 'Stop' or 'Go',

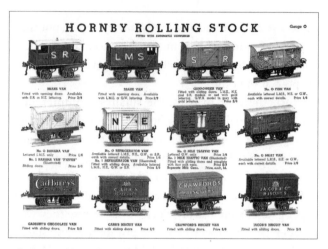

HORNBY ROLLING STOCK
FITTED WITH AUTOMATIC COUPLINGS

Gauge O

BRAKE VAN
Fitted with opening doors. Available with S.R. or N.E. lettering.

BRAKE VAN
Fitted with opening doors. Available with L.M.S. or G.W. lettering. Price 2/9

GUNPOWDER VAN
Fitted with sliding doors. L.M.S., N.E. and S.R. models in red with gold lettering. G.W.R. model in grey with gold lettering.
Price 2/9

No. O FISH VAN
Available lettered L.M.S, N.E. or G.W. each with correct details. Price 1/6

No. O BANANA VAN
Lettered L.M.S. only Price 1/6
No. 1 BANANA VAN 'FYFFES' (Illustrated)
Sliding doors. Price 2/3

No. O REFRIGERATOR VAN
Available lettered L.M.S., N.E., G.W. or S.R. each with correct details. Price 1/6
No. 1 REFRIGERATOR VAN (Illustrated)
Fitted with sliding doors. Available lettered L.M.S., N.E., G.W. or S.R. Price 2/0

No. O MILK TRAFFIC VAN
Lettered G.W. only.
No. 1 MILK TRAFFIC VAN (Illustrated)
Fitted with sliding doors and complete with four milk cans.
Separate Milk Cans. Price 2/3
Price, each, 2d.

No. O MEAT VAN
Available lettered L.M.S., N.E. or G.W. each with correct details. Price 1/6

CADBURY'S CHOCOLATE VAN
Fitted with sliding doors. Price 2/3

CARR'S BISCUIT VAN
Fitted with sliding doors. Price 2/3

CRAWFORD'S BISCUIT VAN
Fitted with sliding doors. Price 2/3

JACOB'S BISCUIT VAN
Fitted with sliding doors. Price 2/3

What boy could resist buying these interesting model railway vans?
(Hornby catalogue 1939)

your breath on the membrane would stop or release the clockwork motor.) A garage could be purchased for this particular car with doors which could be opened by turning a handle, or by pulling on a telephone wire, or just replacing the telephone handset. The outbreak of war in September 1939 meant that these delightful German toys became unavailable.

Some of the larger tinplate toys had electric lights powered from a battery clipped to their base, but generally, batteries did not play a big part in toys of this era because of the cost of their replacement. They were necessary of course when searchlights became popular in 1939 and I also needed one for my torch with which I could signal in red, white or green.

For children who liked making things, Meccano was brilliant and many an engineer started life with it, initially copying a plan and then designing their own models. For those who preferred wood, fretwork sets were available. Fretwork was a hobby which combined profit with pleasure. The initial outlay was practically the only expense involved. The basic necessities required were a steel hand frame, saw blades, a few files, a drill with bits, some pieces of sandpaper and a saw table and clamp. These were used to cut designs in wood.

Another profitable hobby was sealing-wax craft, a hobby which lent itself to the most beautiful ornamental decoration. Basic items required were a few sticks of variously coloured wax, a methylated spirit lamp, a moulder and a spatula. The lamp could be made from a discarded screw-top face cream jar by piercing a hole in the top to admit a wick. The wax could be shaped into leaves and flowers and perhaps added to a matchbox holder; grapes could be added to trinket boxes.

Other types of constructional toys were also available. Brickplayer enabled a child to construct a building using real bricks and a dissoluble cement; similarly, there was Minibrix: interlocking rubber bricks comparable to the Lego of today.

Aircraft were becoming more of an everyday sight and fascinated some children who purchased kits to build models, either for display or to actually fly. Kits were also available for making model lorries.

Scale models of 1930s aircraft. (Hamley's 1938 catalogue)

Minic model vehicles. (Hamley's 1938 catalogue)

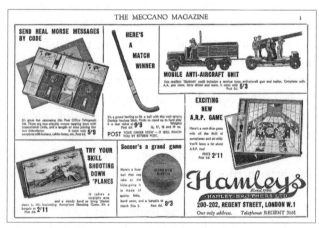

Hamley's suggested wartime games. (*The Meccano Magazine*, November 1939)

During this decade, many municipal parks had ponds on which miniature boats could be sailed, or propelled by clockwork or steam.

Girls and some boys liked to play with dolls, especially those that did something like closing their eyes when laid down, said 'Mama' or wet themselves. Dolls' houses, too, provided hours of entertainment and could be created by an enterprising father from a wooden or cardboard box with home-made furniture inside and, if finances allowed, some small china cups and saucers purchased. Girls also enjoyed playing at being nurses.

A popular and inexpensive present was a set of wax crayons which I never really liked because my pictures always looked messy; I much preferred the more expensive pencil sort of crayon. There were also 'magic' colouring books which had special ink forming the pictures so that when you drew a wet brush across it, the black ink transformed into various colours.

Favourite story books of the decade were those written by Captain W.E. Johns (*Biggles*), Richmal Crompton (*Just William*) and Arthur Ransome (*Swallows and Amazons*) and Frederick Marryat (*Children of the New Forest*), while Palgrave's *Golden Treasury* was a mine for poetry lovers. The *Rupert Bear* series of books and annuals, and the stories written by Enid Blyton, appealed to younger children.

I remember being most impressed by the Arthur Ransome books, so much so that on our long walks to school and back, I instituted with my friends the custom of telling to the others the story we were reading from our library book at that time. Often, we all waited eagerly for the next instalment of the story a friend was reading and telling us about each day.

In pre-war days, an aunt had bought me *Tiny Tots* each week and a friend lent me Enid Blyton's *Sunny Stories*. With the onset of war, to conserve paper, comics and magazines had to be ordered so that only those required would be printed. I managed to get in an order for *The Meccano Magazine* and bought comics occasionally but more often was given or lent them. My favourites were the *Dandy*, the *Beano*, the *Wizard* and the *Knockout* comics (my mother disliked this latter title, thinking it not very nice).

Easy card games such as 'Snap' were popular, while for those with a higher intelligence quotient there was 'Lexicon'. Each card bore a letter of the alphabet and the player was required to make words from the cards held. Apart from the usual board games such as 'Ludo', 'Snakes & Ladders' and 'Draughts', 'Monopoly' became the sensation of the decade. Another popular table game was 'Bagatelle'. A spring propelled a steel ball to the top of a sloping frame where it would roll down into various numbered enclosures staked out by pins. 'Tiddleywinks' was entertaining as it involved flicking plastic counters into a pot, and making something move or jump is always satisfactory. Some children enjoyed playing dominoes and table tennis, although this wasn't really practical if you lived in a crowded house or tenement.

I was fond of reading and longed for the time when I was 7 and thus old enough to qualify for a library ticket. When I took my first book out, I was rather terrified by a label stuck on the inside of the rear cover which said that if you had a communicable disease the book had to be returned not to the library but to the medical officer of health. This care for my welfare should have calmed rather than frightened me, but for some reason it did not. It was the thought that it may have been touched by someone with a dreadful disease but not been disinfected properly and I might catch something horrible which made me so concerned.

Having a library book issued was rather more complicated than in these electronic days. When joining, I was given two library tickets, a red one for fiction and a blue one for non-fiction. When I selected a book, I took it to the counter where the librarian would remove a small card giving its details, and slip it into a pocket on the front of my library ticket, which would then be filed in a long drawer, one for each day. The book would be stamped with the date by which it had to be returned.

When I took the book back to the library, the librarian could see from the date stamp which drawer my ticket would be filed in, take it out, give me my ticket and replace the information card in the book before returning it to the shelves. Sometimes they would have misplaced my ticket and I was asked to select another book while they looked for it.

By the 1930s, *The Illustrated London News* had given readers a visual record of events for almost a century, but its cost was beyond the pockets of the average person. At the end of the decade, *Picture Post* devised a formula for creating something similar with mass appeal at a fraction of the price and flourished throughout the war, but ceased publication in 1957.

For those who liked activities in the company of others, Guides and Brownies, Cubs and Scouts were highly popular groups. For lads with a more religious interest, there was the Boys' Brigade and its junior version, the Life Boys. In addition to Bible study, there were concerts and slide shows, while shoulder badges could be earned for such activities as first aid and signalling; the latter used two flags for semaphore and one for the Morse code.

Some commercial firms organised children's clubs. The Ovaltine drink company operated The League of Ovaltineys, issuing a highly desirable badge to wear. An *Official Rule Book* was issued which made a member feel very special because, on the cover, it

League of Ovaltineys rule book. (Author's collection)

bore the notice: 'WARNING! This book is strictly private. It contains confidential rules and secrets intended for members of The League of Ovaltineys only. If lost, the finder is requested to return it, WITHOUT OPENING, to the owner whose name is on the back cover.'

Every member was expected to learn and keep seven golden rules, the first being, 'I promise to do the things my parents tell me to – because they know what's best for me and I want them to be proud of me.'

Other promises were about getting plenty of exercise, studying hard at school, getting lots of good, sound sleep and eating vegetables and fruit because they were good for you. Then there were secret passwords, door knocks and signs to use when greeting fellow members. Last but not least, we enjoyed our own weekly programme on Radio Luxembourg, starting and ending with our very own song. Radio Luxembourg, which ran from 1933 until 1992, was one of the earliest commercial radio stations broadcasting to Great Britain.

The national daily paper, the *News Chronicle*, ran the Arkubs based on a daily strip story relating the adventures of Mr and Mrs Noah, Shem, Ham and Japhet, the latter being the principal bosun and chief executive officer. The Arkub badge had a smile, 'because all true Arkubs keep smiling'. A boy Arkub was to wear his badge on the left side of his coat or shirt, while girl Arkubs wore theirs on the right side of their coats or frocks. A secret code was provided for communication and if you introduced six new members you were rewarded with a breakfast set.

Standing orders, otherwise known as 'The Bosun's Pipes for Arkubs', said that they must always be truthful, help each other and help other people. When on holiday, if possible, they must 'help each other to enjoy themselves, exercise together, go for walks together and have games on the sands or in the fields'.

The standard amount of pocket money was about a penny a week, but by using your imagination, you could increase it, perhaps by mowing lawns and brushing paths. One father of twins was very crafty. Having bought a new lawnmower, he called his sons together and said, 'Now I want to make it quite clear; no one is to use the mower except me.'

The twins looked at the shiny green and red machine and longed to touch it. 'Dad, if we promise to look after it very carefully, may we use it to cut the lawns?'

'Well you heard what I said and the answer is "NO!"'

'But, dad, if we both promise to use it ever so carefully, as a very special favour, do you think we might give it a push?'

'Well alright as long as you really do take very special care.'

'Thanks very much dad, we will.' So the smart father got the result he'd been angling for! His lawns were cut willingly and for no payment.

Butchers usually had a bike with a carrier on the front and employed lads, particularly on Saturdays, to deliver the Sunday joint, so this was a job available for a smart boy.

In the thirties, tradespeople were always willing to deliver bulky articles without charge. One day, for instance, my grandfather took me to a department store and bought me the figure of eight *autobahn* I mentioned earlier. The shop promised to deliver it. We travelled to my grandfather's house by electric tram and within about an hour of our arrival a van delivered our purchase!

Scottish children were lucky because, if travelling by train, they didn't have to lug around their parents' shopping. Railways north of the border adopted a useful shop parcel system which was never taken up in England.

At a station, a passenger could buy a packet of labels priced at a penny each. A perforation ran through the centre of each label and when an item was purchased, half of this label was stuck on to the purchased item which was delivered to the station cloakroom. When you finished your shopping, you went to the station cloakroom and, on presenting the ticket stub you had retained, you were handed your parcels.

There were no supermarkets in the thirties and, consequently, there were more specialist shops such as grocer's, fishmonger's and greengrocer's. Most children enjoyed looking around Woolworths, which could be found in any town, selling articles priced at 3*d* and 6*d*. Items children found particularly attractive in Woolworths were sweets, toys, jokes and magic tricks. As all Woolworths stores were laid out to the same design, when you were away and went into one of their shops, it felt as if you were back at home – that is until you heard one of the shop assistants speaking in a different accent.

Photography was relatively expensive at this time, both for the initial cost of the camera and then for the developing and printing. It was therefore out of most children's reach. Initially, it was a black and white world; colour film was available in the thirties but was very expensive, especially as most cameras took 2½-inch by 3½-inch negatives or larger. It was in that decade that the first 35-millimetre cameras were made. They were very expensive and cost about £40 (sixteen weeks' wages for the average working man), but had the great advantage that the narrow film they used could be bought in bulk, loaded into a cassette. It was therefore cheap to run compared with the wider film with backing paper required for the larger cameras. These miniature cameras were also better at taking pictures in confined spaces. Usually, most families were able to purchase an inexpensive box camera and use it for holiday snaps.

Home movies became popular in this decade; some households owned a 9.5-millimetre silent projector and hired films. If, however, you were rather better off, you might actually have owned a movie camera and produced films of your holidays to show your friends who would be impressed, not only because you could take films, but also by your choice of holiday.

We were a very 'green' decade because we didn't use electricity from the mains or batteries for our entertainment and we spent more of our leisure in the open air.

Speedway racing of motorcycles was an exciting new sport which had started in Australia and the USA before the First World War. As a dirt track was used, the specialist machines, having only one gear and no brakes, went broadside into bends. The first British speedway meeting was in 1927 and the first British match race championship was held in 1931 and won by Vic Huxley. In this decade, many of the larger cities in Great Britain installed tracks for this dramatic activity and probably another for greyhound racing, which also could be enjoyed for an affordable sum.

Ice hockey, which evolved from stick-and-ball games played in Britain in the eighteenth century, became very popular in countries which had a lot of snow in the winter, but very few cities in Britain found it economic to have an ice rink at this time so the sport did not develop much.

Record shops provided entertainment as you could ask for a record and then play it in a soundproof cubicle to see whether you liked it and then decide whether to buy it or not. Most towns had at least one music shop selling records.

Soap-box trolleys were desirable, especially if you lived in a hilly district where you could use them to descend quickly. Parts for construction were widely available: a wooden box, wheels from an old pram, a length of cord for steering the front wheels and a stick to rub against a rear wheel to form a brake. Apart from providing hours of fun, it could be a very useful money-spinner, particularly if you lived at a seaside resort. Holidaymakers would be very pleased to pay you for transporting their cases from the station to their boarding house. If you were really ingenious, you might have been able to temporarily remove its wheels and convert your trolley into a sledge, or you might have preferred a purpose-built one. If you were small, a tin tea tray formed a ready-made sledge and could also be used throughout the year for sliding down slag heaps found adjacent to coal mines.

Then there was the cinema. Talkies had just come in; most of the films were in black and white but a few, very few, were actually in colour. These included the Mickey Mouse series and then the full-length *Snow White and the Seven Dwarfs*. For railway enthusiasts, there were three black and white films released in the 1930s: *The Ghost Train*, *Kate Plus Ten* and *Oh Mr Porter*.

The Ghost Train was written by the actor Arnold Ridley who went to junior school with my mother and the same grammar school as me, although many years earlier. Ridley was also well known for playing Private Godfrey in the television series *Dad's Army*. *The Ghost Train*, made in 1931, starred Jack Hulbert and Cicely Courtneidge. The filming at Camerton, just south of Bath, proved such a great attraction that as many as 5,000 spectators travelled from Bath and Bristol to watch the night shots being taken, some actually remaining all through the night. Filming also took place at Box

Tunnel, Bramley, on the Reading to Basingstoke branch, and at Somerton and Barmouth.

1937 saw two railway films released, the best being *Oh Mr Porter* starring Will Hay. Scenes were shot at Cliddesden, which had been closed to passengers on 12 September 1932. One morning, the film unit arrived at the station and found two old women sitting on a station seat waiting for a train. When told that trains had ceased running five years earlier and that the station was now part of a film set, one of the old women let rip. The more the crew insisted it was not a real station, the more she insisted that she would write to *The Times* about it!

The third railway film of the decade was the Edgar Wallace thriller *Kate Plus Ten*, whose night scenes were shot at Dunkerton Colliery Sidings, south of Bath, in November 1937.

Film stars of the decade included Shirley Temple, Googie Withers, Charlie Chaplin, Stan Laurel, Oliver Hardy, Arthur Lucan (Old Mother Riley), John Wayne, James Mason, Arthur Askey and Richard (Stinker) Murdoch.

Many people liked to spend Saturday afternoons supporting their local football team. They weren't dressed quite the same as today because their shorts were longer and their jerseys didn't sport advertisements. The rules of football were slightly different then: you could pass the ball back to the goalie who could use both their hands and feet. There was no punishment for passing the ball back to the goalkeeper, whereas today a goalie can touch it with their feet but not their hands if it is kicked back to them. The Cup Final at Wembley in 1939 between Wolverhampton Wanderers and Portsmouth was the last until the end of the war in 1945 because of the need to minimise the number of passengers travelling. If you're wondering, Portsmouth were the winners! To raise money to support your team, you could buy a penny ticket and be in a lottery to win the ball at the end of the match. Programmes made of flimsy paper were on sale for one penny; those with foresight kept them and, today, they can be sold for many times the original cover price.

Most football grounds had terraces at each end and usually, on the lower tiers along each side, most spectators stood. With hooliganism rising in the 1970s, some top-division football grounds introduced all-seater stadia, but since, as many supporters prefer to stand, new stadia have been built for football and rugby which have safe standing areas. The answer seems to be rail seats where each metal seat is incorporated within a robust metal frame that forms a waist-high rail for the spectators behind, so with a barrier along every row, dangerous surging is impossible. The disadvantage is that, due to the higher cost of providing seating, the number of teenagers attending is lower.

As more people could afford a car, caravans drawn by cars rather than horses were all the rage in the thirties as, once bought, they provided a cheap holiday as you only needed to offer a farmer a few shillings to park your caravan in one of their fields for a week. Until the thirties, most people able to afford one could also have afforded a hotel, which was why they had not been popular before. Even cheaper was camping with a tent, but this wasn't so warm and was less rainproof. When war broke out in 1939, we were on a camping holiday. After returning to our tent, we discovered that the police had been through our belongings to check that we weren't German spies. An early ruling in 1939 was that white tents had to be painted green so as to be invisible from the air.

Apart from pets such as cats and dogs, many people kept budgerigars. For the elderly and lonely – remember television had yet to be made available for all – they provided something to look at and talk to.

Youth hostelling became very popular at this time, providing a cheap bed for those willing to move about the country under their own steam. There was far less mobility in the thirties than there is today and it was quite likely that grandparents, uncles and aunts would be living nearby. This was useful because if you had a problem, perhaps needing childcare, a shoulder to cry on or just a helping hand, you could call on the rest of the family for help.

Bonfire Night or Guy Fawkes' Night – 'the Fifth of November' – was as exciting in the thirties as it is today, but it was celebrated more on a street basis or by your family rather than as a large, organised event. As money for buying fireworks was scarce, many children made a man out of old clothes, called a 'guy', placed him in an old pram and pushed it round the streets hoping that passers-by would be impressed by their efforts and offer a donation.

Materials for the bonfire were collected well in advance and in some cases had to be guarded in case a rival gang stole your combustibles or lit the fire in advance as a joke.

There was much more respect for keeping fireworks exclusive to the Fifth of November at this time. In fact I was told you could be fined for letting off fireworks on another night. Certainly, it is unfair for those who keep animals who are terrified of fireworks who have to take precautions for a week either side of the actual night.

Squibs seemed the most popular type of firework as they were cheap to buy and it was fun watching people jump out of their way and not know where the explosives would jump to next. Rockets launched from bottles provided good value and, if you were given returnable bottles, the cash you received from them could be used to buy more rockets and you could actually launch them from a borrowed milk bottle. Catherine wheels, golden rains and other pretty fireworks were thought to be for toddlers.

When I was 5 years old, I held a firework party. A friend I invited kept asking me, 'Will there be any bangers?' to which I said, 'Yes.' Then came the Fifth of November. After tea we waited with great excitement for my father to come home at about 6.15 p.m. When he did, we trooped out into the garden and the display commenced with a banger. This caused my friend to burst into tears. He was taken inside and consoled by my grandmother who was enjoying the event from the safety, comfort and warmth of the house.

Nearly all racehorses travelled by rail in the thirties. If the demand was sufficient, a special train would be made for the horseboxes, each of which had a groom's compartment at one end, or else they would be attached to the end of a suitable passenger train where they would be detached at the station nearest to the race course and the animals then walked to their destination. Similar arrangements would be made for return to their home stables. Bertram Mills' circus was also transported by train.

Three

FOOD, DRINK AND SWEETS

In the thirties, most families only had just about enough money to live on and so economised wherever possible. Meals therefore were cooked at home and only as a very special treat were fish-and-chip suppers brought home or eaten out. If your house had a garden, usually the front garden was just for flowers and a lawn, with another small lawn in the back garden, but most of the land at the rear was used for growing vegetables. If you didn't have a garden, or if you wished to supplement it, an allotment was an alternative.

Most food was home cooked, apart from bread. A housewife made and was proud of her cakes and jams, believing it to be a failing to use 'boughten' food, something only done by lazy housewives. In Scotland, many economical lunches consisted of tatties and mince, followed by custard and a dab of jam or Golden Syrup.

Sometimes neighbours could be a nuisance. One man had a plum tree at the bottom of his garden and beyond the fence was a railway cutting. One day, a gang of railwaymen cut the grass, left it to dry and then burnt it, unfortunately scorching the plum tree; the man claimed compensation from the railway company.

The following year, he asked the railwaymen to repeat the exercise as he said it had helped his tree bear a more bountiful crop than usual.

Another cheap source of food were hens, which could be kept for their eggs and meat, and rabbits, kept just for their meat. Children were encouraged not to name them and get too friendly – it might be acceptable to eat an egg laid by Jemima, but a different matter altogether to actually eat her.

Neighbours could cause problems with hen houses. A great-uncle of mine lived next door to an engine driver who wanted to benefit from his job and offload some 'free' coal. As his engine passed the end of his garden, he arranged for a very large lump of coal to be placed on the footplate and then, as he went by, he would 'accidentally' kick the coal off the engine. It should have rolled down the embankment, gone 'ping' through the wire fence and landed in his garden.

However, 'there's many a slip 'twixt cup and lip': the plan did not quite work. The coal bumped down the embankment, went ping through the fence, but the driver failed to get his geometry right and it pinged through the wrong fence and punched a hole in my great-uncle's hen house.

When my great-uncle saw the coal and the hole, he realised what had happened so when the driver came home from his shift, he made him repair the damage.

It was not unknown for people who were having a hard time, if they were fortunate enough to have a railway at the bottom of their garden, to get a free supply of coal by setting up a large board with the face of a cat painted on it, with the mouth being a large hole. It was too tempting for young firemen not to show off their prowess and aim a lump through the hole.

Most hot beverages in the thirties were tea, coffee or a cheap bottled liquid coffee substitute called 'Camp Coffee' which provided an occasional change. At elevenses or in the evening, cocoa might have been drunk, or if you were well off, Ovaltine, Bournvita or Horlicks.

Sweet shops were a great place to spend your Saturday penny. In the window were jars and jars of delicious, mouth-watering sweets; it was difficult to choose, you wanted them all. You might have been rash and spent all your money on one type. The shopkeeper would take the jar down from the shelf and fill a paper bag shaped like a miniature inverted dunce's cap. Alternatively, you could buy a farthing's worth of four kinds of sweets. Barley sugars were my favourite; I liked both their colour and taste. There were also acid drops, gobstoppers, humbugs, aniseed balls, liquorice sticks, sherbet, dolly mixtures, love hearts, pear drops, sugared almonds, jelly babies and toffee.

Towards the end of the decade, some wrapped boiled sweets were available from the jars, but most were unwrapped. Wine gums, blocks of chocolate (the texture of Aero gave you a wonderful sensation when sucking it), Milky Ways and Mars Bars all came wrapped.

In the summer, a man on a tricycle would come round selling either Wall's or Eldorado ice cream and this was a treat indeed for very few homes could afford a refrigerator. If you were a frequent purchaser of Wall's ice cream, you could ask for a card with a large 'W' to place in your window when you wanted the passing tricyclist to call. This saved you having to look out for him and his trike, which announced 'Stop Me and Buy One' on the front.

Lack of refrigeration caused problems with milk. Our dairyman had his own cows which he milked twice a day, so twice daily, he delivered the milk. Initially, he brought it round on foot wearing a yoke with a milk can chain suspended on either side. Using the appropriate measure, he would ladle the quantity my mother desired into a jug left on the back doorstep, the back door being the equivalent of a mansion's tradesmen's entrance.

A little later in the decade, he upgraded his transport to a motorbike with sidecar, and later still to a van. Other milkmen used carts, either the three- or four-wheeled variety, pushed by hand or propelled. The Co-op was very modern and had a Morrisson electric milk float in which the driver sat and steered.

A selection of toys from Tri-ang, including a toy Wall's ice cream tricycle.
(Hamley's 1938 catalogue)

In the interests of even better hygiene, in the mid-thirties our milkman changed to supplying milk in bottles containing a half pint, pint or quart. These were capped with a card top with a centre which could be easily pushed out to insert a finger to pull off the top. Normally, the top had the name of the dairy on it but just before Christmas I always grew excited when, instead of the usual top, it was decorated with holly.

On a very hot day, my mother always scalded the milk soon after its arrival to prevent it from turning sour. Another method she used was to place a milk bottle-shaped piece of earthenware over it. This was kept damp and the evaporation kept the milk cool and, incidentally, taught me a little science.

Meat was kept in a meat safe, which was a metal box, the walls of which were perforated to allow a breeze to waft through yet keep out the flies. Flies seemed more plentiful in the thirties and I remember having great fun using the curtains to trap them against the glass and then squashing them.

The baker called every day in his motor van, while the grocer came every Tuesday morning to receive the weekly order from my mother and it would be delivered that afternoon. If I saw the grocer's boy coming with a heavy box of groceries, I always rushed to the back door to open it for him and say, 'Good afternoon.' He was always rather puzzled as to whether he should first say, 'Good afternoon' or thank me for opening the door.

Hovis advertisement, May 1939.

The butcher delivered the meat ordered weekly. This was particularly exciting for me because, if asked politely, he would run and jump over the gate. He did this once too often and, at someone else's house, broke his leg. I was able to repay him for this entertainment when I grew too big for my pedal car. Initially, the problem was overcome by my father fixing a block of wood on the seat so that my knees were higher, but eventually I was just too big to fit in.

Just before Christmas one year, the butcher noticed this unused car on the back lawn and said that his young son was longing for a pedal car, but that frankly he could not afford a new one and asked if he could buy mine cheaply. My father suggested that I should be generous and let him have it for a nominal sum, so I agreed and felt nice inside for doing so.

Because most housewives made their own cakes and pastries rather than bought them ready-made, children had the fun of scraping out a bowl of uncooked cake mixture. Similarly, housewives made their own jams, so the preserving pan needed to be cleared of any leftovers.

I remember on one occasion my mother had left eight or so pots of gooseberry jam to cool. I felt it necessary to test the quality, so dipped a finger in. It tasted good! I wondered if it was all of the same quality and felt the question needed to be answered. Eventually, I ate the equivalent of almost half a pot of gooseberry jam and was nearly sick. Although it was of excellent quality, I was put off eating gooseberry jam for years.

In late summer, many households went to the hedgerows to pick blackberries to make jam, although the younger members probably felt it necessary to taste some of the berries so did not place as many in the basket as the adults.

Fishwives were seen in some towns. In Dundee, for example, dressed in striped aprons, they came by train from Arbroath and, on arrival, walked to their allotted selling spot carrying fish 'smokies' in wicker baskets held on their front by a broad band over their necks.

Tinned food, being more expensive than fresh, was usually kept for special occasions and emergencies. As a small boy I once caused my parents considerable embarrassment. My grandfather took us all to Cheddar for a strawberry tea. As I ate it, I observed, 'These aren't as nice as tinned strawberries, are they?' The reason was that tinned strawberries had more sugar than the fresh ones on my plate and as a young child I adored sweet things.

A seasonal sight was French onion sellers going round on bikes with strings of onions. As a lad I thought it couldn't have been economic to come over from France just to sell a few onions, not realising that they had brought over many more onions which were being kept in a depot.

Quite a number of my friends and I were given a daily spoonful of cod liver oil to keep us healthy. Some found it rather sickly, but I enjoyed taking it. One day, one of my cousins, whose mother was having a baby, came to stay for a few days and, as he was rather weak, brought a tin of glucose to build him up. He seemed to enjoy taking his daily spoonful, so I thought I'd see what it tasted like. It was sweet; it was good, so I stole a few more spoonfuls when I thought no one was looking.

Many children enjoyed four meals a day: breakfast, dinner, tea and supper, bread being present at all or most of them since it was relatively cheap and filling. Breakfast could be porridge or cereal, followed by bread or toast, with marmalade spread on it, the marmalade made by Mum from Seville oranges which appeared in the shops early in the new year. Children in poor homes may have just had bread and dripping for breakfast. If you were very lucky you might have been given a boiled egg with bread soldiers to dip in. Mid-morning there might have been a drink, very often a cup of cocoa or Camp Coffee, and perhaps a biscuit if you'd been good. Then there was dinner, generally the main meal of the day. The first course would be potatoes, vegetables and, on Mondays and Tuesdays, the meat left over from the Sunday joint, then perhaps sausages, toad-in-the-hole, cottage pie or liver on Wednesdays and Thursdays and fish on Fridays. If meat was too expensive, a meatless stew could be made with vegetables and gravy. This course would be followed by some form of sweet, perhaps stewed apple and custard. Most factory and office workers returned home for this repast during the hour they were given off work. They missed out on tea of bread and jam which those at home were able to enjoy, the jam of course being made by Mum in summer from the soft fruits available. If you'd been good and the family finances could afford it, there would also be some cake, again made by Mum. Following Dad's return from work in the evening, there would be supper, rather like the first course of the midday meal, but simpler – often something on toast, egg and chips, or fish and chips. Dripping from the Sunday roast provided a scrumptious supper on bread or toast for a few evenings, the toast being made by holding the bread on a toasting fork in front of the fire. The fire was also used for roasting chestnuts – the edible kind of course, not horse chestnuts. On Sundays when you were not rushing off to work or school and had more time to eat your breakfast, many families had a full breakfast of bacon, egg, fried bread and perhaps a sausage or black pudding.

The general hours for factory workers were 8 a.m. until 12.30 p.m. and then 1.30 p.m. until 6 p.m. Often a hooter marked the end of the shift as not everyone owned a watch. It was useful, too, for those working outside, such as road menders or road sweepers, to know that it was time for their midday break. As factory workers were not given time for elevenses, they sometimes took a sandwich with them and ate it when they had a spare moment.

Because most households did not own a refrigerator, this meant that for perishable food like meat, fish, vegetables and fruit, the housewife had to shop every few days or send a child on an errand.

Rabbit was a cheap source of meat in the thirties – before the onset of myxomatosis, a disease that first appeared in Britain in the 1950s – and was freely available, caught either officially or by poachers. A snare could be set in a 'run' – a regular rabbit path – or by placing a large net over the rabbit holes and sending in a ferret to chase them out. This was quite an important industry in some parts of the country. During the season, for example, several van loads of rabbits were carried daily on the Barnstaple to Taunton line.

Some food common in the thirties is rarely seen now, examples being a bowl of bread and milk – simple to make; while junket, sweetened curds of milk as devoured by Little Miss Muffet when she was seated on her tuffet, often appeared at children's parties. Tripe and onions, although having an obnoxious appearance, was both delicious and nutritious; the same was true of chitterling, the cooked, smaller intestines of pigs.

Smith's crisps were a popular snack, the bag containing a twist of blue paper filled with salt to add if you so desired.

My maternal grandfather owned a grocer's shop. Sugar was sold loose – no, not literally loose, you weren't offered a handful of it, but my grandfather received it in sacks and bagged it for his customers. One man who was anxious to get his money's worth always asked for 2 pounds of sugar in a 1-pound bag. He noticed that my grandfather placed an empty bag on the scales and then filled it until the scales registered 2 pounds, so having 2 pounds in a 1-pound bag meant that he was given slightly more sugar – the difference in weight between a paper 1-pound and 2-pound bag. Unless he was very careful carrying it home, anything that he gained by this ploy was probably lost in spillage due to the fact that the top couldn't be bent over because the bag was so full.

Biscuits, too, were sold loose, broken ones being kept aside and sold cheaper. Treacle came in a large drum and when, one day, the grocer's boy failed to turn the tap off and it flooded the floor, my grandfather was not too happy.

Bacon and ham were both served from a large joint placed on a meat slicer, and were sliced by turning a handle which spun a sharp wheel. I always thought it was a task fraught with danger and could imagine it was all too easy to cut off a finger. My grandfather provided chairs for customers so that they could sit while ordering the goods they desired and while he was taking them from the shelves. On a Saturday, as some of his customers were not paid until that evening and didn't have the wherewithal to pay for the groceries until then, my grandfather had to stay open until midnight.

Four

SCHOOL LIFE

School life in the thirties was rather different from today. As there was relatively little traffic on the roads, it was safe a few weeks after a child started school at 5 years of age – pre-school classes were unusual – for that child to walk to school on their own and, if the road outside the school was busy, a warden assisted children across. The one stationed by my infant school carried a board saying, 'Danger: Children Crossing'. It was ambiguous. Were the motorists or the children in danger?

Until I started school, being an only child I'd hardly mixed with other children. I should have been taught how to make friends, how to share, to realise that other people may have different ideas, warned that not every-one is nice and how to fight.

School hours were 9 a.m. until noon and 2 p.m. until 4.15 p.m., with a ten-minute break mid-morning and mid-afternoon. No school meals were provided until after the beginning of the Second World War, so children went home for lunch, or 'dinner' as we called it then, but the few children who lived too far from school to go home brought sandwiches. Most mothers didn't go out to work and were able to cook a midday meal and most husbands returned home too, unless their employment was such that it was impossible.

This meant that my friends and I got plenty of exercise: walking 1¼ miles to school in the morning, 1¼ miles home for lunch, 1¼ miles back for afternoon school and then 1¼ miles home for tea. If it was raining, we used the tram, but generally we walked because our parents could not have afforded the penny fare for each journey. The first school I attended only taught boys up to 7 years of age. The transfer to junior school involved a walk of 1¾ miles each way twice daily. It taught us independence: we could not rely on others to see that we arrived at school on time – it was up to us, and if we encountered

The author in his school uniform. (G.T. Maggs)

any problems on the way, we had to solve them; there was no mobile phone to seek help.

Not infrequently, boys and girls had different entrances to a school, although by the thirties they tended to use the same way in, although often they went to separate playgrounds, which was sensible as boys were encouraged to rush around playing rough games, while girls did gentler activities with ropes and tennis balls.

The class size was about sixty. We sat on fold-up bench seats, two to a desk, in rows, all facing the front. Often a teacher would place a girl next to a boy, which tended to inhibit talking as two boys or two girls together tended to encourage chatting. The desks had sloping tops which could be opened to give access to space for storing books, pens and pencils. It was not unknown for an unwell child, unable to reach the lavatory in time, to lift the lid and be sick inside the desk. If there were chairs, rather than bench seats, this provided an opportunity for a child to stoop down, carefully untie another's shoe lace and then re-tie it round a chair leg. It was a particularly simple act to perform on a child who was engrossed in reading or solving a mathematical problem.

As class sizes were so large, teaching had to be teacher-centred, rather than child-centred learning, with quite a lot taught by rote. Infant and junior schools were generally mixed, but senior schools tended to be single sex. I think that a mixed class changed the natural dynamics somewhat, the boys tending to be less boisterous and the girls kinder.

As men were considered to be the breadwinners, boys would be taught woodwork, metalwork and engineering drawing to prepare them for future working lives. Conversely, women were considered homemakers and the girls would learn cookery and needlework to prepare them for married life, with typing on the syllabus in case they ever needed to get a job. It was a pity that boys were also not taught to type for it would have been a useful skill to have acquired.

White chalk on a blackboard and easel were used by the teacher for writing words and drawing, the board being cleaned with a duster – washed weekly – rather than cleaned by a special blackboard rubber which may not have been invented at that time. Children thought it a great honour to be asked by the teacher to go up and clean the board, failing to realise that it kept dust away from the teacher and prevented them from catching silicosis.

Unless a teacher was very charismatic, she (and in infant and junior schools, the teacher was generally female) had to be strict or it would have been chaotic. Knuckle-rapping with a ruler was the treatment for mis-behaviour and deemed to be reasonably acceptable; it didn't hurt too much, but was enough to persuade you to keep to the straight and narrow. For serious offences, the headmaster used the cane, but this made only an occasional appearance. Corporal punishment was unfair because some pupils were less sensitive and could endure more pain than others, or some might have felt less humiliated in that situation than their peers, yet teachers punished them equally. Similarly, if punishment was not immediate, it led to anguish, and some pupils felt that more keenly than others. Even if the punishment was unjust, it was not acceptable to argue with the teacher, you just had to accept it.

The best teachers rarely needed to punish pupils because their students caught their enthusiasm for the subject and actually wanted to pay attention. In order for a teacher to command a good view of the class, they sat on a high chair behind a tall desk with both red and black inkwells.

After registration, we trooped into the hall to sing a hymn, hear a prayer and any announcements before returning to our classrooms for scripture, followed by arithmetic until break. After break, there would be, in varying order, perhaps English, geography, history and singing. There was very little physical education or games, although very occasionally we walked half a mile to the park for cricket. At my junior school we had no sports day, nor any swimming lessons; the omission of the latter proved fatal to one of my school friends who fell into the river and drowned. One afternoon a week, the boys learnt handwork while the girls learnt sewing, older girls designing their own patterns for needlework. For convenience, two classes joined together for this lesson, one teacher taking all the boys and the other all the girls.

I wasn't very good at handwork, most things failing to fit properly or coming unstuck. One thing I did enjoy was papier mâché. I made a dish with plasticine and then lined the inside with layers of torn-up newspaper soaked in paste. When this dried, the plasticine was carefully peeled off and the newspaper hardened to be quite solid.

Probably due to a shortage of funds, most of the text-books were old and well worn; I can't remember ever having a new book in infant or junior school. What was interesting and unusual was that standing up and looking through the window (windows were deliberately set high to prevent pupils wasting time looking out), if reading a book printed by the Pitman Press, I could look out across the road to where that book had actually been printed.

I remember one particularly funny incident: a teacher was walking round his class engaged in writing composition. He spotted some liquid under a pupil's desk. 'What's your name boy?' he demanded. 'Leakey, sir,' came the reply. 'That doesn't surprise me,' said the master.

If a teacher knew their pupils well and was confident that discipline could be relaxed a little without control being lost, we could all have some fun:

Teacher: Mary, go to the map and find North America.
Mary: Here it is.
Teacher: Good. Now class, who discovered America?
Class: Mary.

Teacher: John, why are you doing your maths multiplications on the floor?

John: Well, Miss, you told me to do them without using tables.

Teacher: Tony, how do you spell crocodile?
Tony: K–R–O–K–O–D–I–A–L.
Teacher: No, that's wrong.
Tony: Maybe it's wrong, but you asked me how *I* spell it.

Here are some more funny anecdotes I recall from my schooldays:

A blizzard is the inside of a foul.

Crematorium is Latin for dairy.

Equinox is derived from two Latin words *Equus* means a horse and *nox* means night, therefore it is a nightmare.

Louis XIV was gelatined.

In our classroom there are many widows, all down on one side.

In the orchard the damsels are ripening splendidly.

Kites are light frames of wood sent into the sky by boys with tails on them.

One smart lad, a Bath Abbey choirboy, devised a clever plan. In the arithmetic lesson he persuaded a friend to go to the teacher and ask, 'Are seven sevens forty-nine?' while he went to the other side of the teacher and asked rather more quietly, 'Please, Sir, can we go home now?' The teacher, hearing only the mathematical question, answered, 'Yes', thus allowing the choirboy to whoop with delight, 'The teacher says we can all go home now!' The class as one, stood up and trooped into the playground, through a door into the corridor and then returned to the classroom, subsequently working better for their trip into the fresh air. With some classes it would have been foolish for a teacher to allow this distraction because, as the saying goes, 'if you give them an inch, they would have taken a yard', which meant that the children might have carried out further tricks, but our wise teacher knew we were aware of the limits and would not overstep them.

Before I started infant school, I listened to the excellent schools programmes on the BBC, expecting to hear those familiar voices when I started school itself. Unfortunately, neither my infant nor junior school had radios and so were unable to make use of those excellent broadcasts.

Monday was 'milk money day'. Most parents availed themselves of the opportunity of buying a third of a pint of milk for their child for the very reasonable sum of 2½d a week. Some children received their milk free – I never was able to work out whether it was because they were poor or not very healthy, but it was probably the latter as their milk tasted horrible because some body-strengthening mixture had been added. Village schools often had their milk supplied by a local farmer.

At first, I drank my milk through a straw and it really was a straw, but in the late thirties, the school changed to a straw made of waxed paper. It wasn't wise to dally over drinking your milk because, if you did, the waxed paper would unravel and then you'd have to do the unthinkable – drink it out of the bottle.

The used milk tops and straws were disposed of in the wastepaper basket and made it smell unpleasant. A teacher would regularly collect the milk tops and wash them and then they would provide material for a handwork lesson.

As they were simply a card disc with a hole in the centre, you could weave coloured raffia over the card and then fix these raffia-covered discs to a card to create a mat which you took home to an admiring parent … who then had to find some use for this rather crude article.

While the teacher was collecting the milk money, we children were kept busy with art using plasticine, chalk pastels or lentils. Being very unimaginative, the only thing I could envisage using my plasticine for was to make a snake.

Some teachers ran an optional savings club and many children paid in sixpence a week towards a 15*s* savings certificate which, after five years, was worth £1. My mother was most impressed by the teacher who had collected 15s from various pupils because she immediately bought a certificate so that it was dated before you had actually paid for it. Thus, by the time you received it, it was already on its way to being a £1.

Many school toilets at the time were set in a block apart from the main building and this caused problems if it was raining. Quite a lot of them had no roof, but because of the unpleasant smell emanating from them, this was a good thing!

A school nurse visited the school regularly for nit inspection. I meekly submitted myself to this, although was never told what she was looking for. Information was much more forthcoming on another occasion when my mother was able to warn me that the following day, at school, I'd receive a 'prick' – an inoculation against some disease.

If you sat at the back – which was where teachers placed children who could be trusted – and your sight was poor, you couldn't always see the writing on the blackboard. With large classes, teachers didn't always spot if you had a sight problem. Similarly, if you had a hearing problem and were at the back, you often missed out. I remember one child who was sent to sit at the back by the teacher because she kept turning round. She was quickly cured because there was nothing of interest to see on the blank wall at the back of the class.

By the 1930s, if a child was left-handed most teachers accepted it, but a few still forced them to write with their right hand.

Most schools supplied their pupils with a pencil, dip pen and blotting paper; pencils were used until a child was about 7 years old and deemed careful enough to be trusted with ink. At the top of the desk was a hole for holding a ceramic inkwell. If you were good, on Monday mornings the teacher may have granted you the important task of going round the room filling the inkwells from a spouted can filled with ink made from dried powder.

Inkwells were a mixed blessing: your enemies could fill your well with blotting paper; also, inkwells supplied a source of material for making ammunition – ink pellets – and if you were a messy sort of person when using ink, especially with a dip pen, it was all too easy to load it with too much ink and make a blot. Incidentally, a well-loaded pen was ideal for flicking at people – preferably those who wore a white shirt or blouse. If you sat behind a girl with pigtails, it was all too tempting to dip the ends in the inkwell!

Many teachers at this time didn't realise that good handwriting was partly a gift and that some children just lacked the ability to control their muscles sufficiently. Such children were able to reach a certain standard but beyond that, no matter how hard they practised, they made no progress. The same applied to learning a musical instrument or playing games – not everyone could be an Olympic gold medalist!

Heating in the first classroom I went to was by coke burnt in a black, cast-iron stove. Once, when my teacher was ill, we went to another room with an open fire guarded by a screen. Within a few weeks of my starting, these fires were replaced by electric fires of the bar variety. These were fixed high on the walls, meaning the reflectors shone heat on to my head, which gave me a headache, so I didn't think they were an improvement at all!

Council schools in the thirties didn't usually require pupils to wear a school uniform, but quite a number of children wore the school badge on their headgear and a school tie on their shirt or blouse.

Two days were particularly memorable in the school year: Empire Day (24 May, Queen Victoria's birthday), when we gathered in the playground and walked round the Union Jack, and Remembrance Day on 11 November when, at 11 a.m., we stood for two minutes' silence.

For exercise, occasionally we had 'drill'. We marched into the playground and then paraded round before getting into lines and performing what I considered useless actions, such as swinging our arms round forwards and then backwards. 'Running on the spot' seemed particularly fatuous; it would have been much more fun to have had to run somewhere! We then had to collect a mat from a pile and lie down on it. We were then instructed to pretend we were riding a bicycle. Again, I considered this a useless activity but did it to humour the teacher. Years after my schooldays, I learnt that 'Those who can, do: those who can't, teach.'

Quite a considerable proportion of classrooms in the thirties had one wall consisting of a wooden screen up to a height of about 5 feet with glass above it. If a larger space was required, the screen could be folded up to make two classrooms into one. The great disadvantage of this screen was that, if the teacher in the adjoining room had a loud voice, you could hear all that was said because the screen was far from soundproof.

It was only years later, when studying the history of education, that I learnt the reason for the screens. In earlier days, classes had been about twice the size and so needed twice the space, but when numbers in classes were reduced, the screens transformed one room into two.

Schools could be very dangerous places. On one occasion, a teacher was *pushing* an upright piano, which was the easier option instead of *pulling* it. Tragically, it toppled over and killed a child. To prevent this happening again, that education authority set all its pianos on a wide framework, making it impossible for them to overbalance. This, however, led to an unfortunate consequence.

The school was designed so that its classrooms led off from a central hall where the piano was normally kept. It could, however, easily be wheeled into any room when required. One day, a new teacher was appointed and was given the room with the only access being through another classroom. Although the doorways of the other rooms were wide enough for the piano and its widened base to pass through, unfortunately the doorway into this particular room was not. The new teacher was the only pianist on the staff! When he wanted to teach a music lesson, he had to borrow someone else's room when they were out engaged with games or physical education.

When it was time to leave junior school, there were a number of options available: grammar school, a central school, or an ordinary senior school. Those hoping to be selected for a grammar school education usually opted to do homework, set and marked by their junior school teacher, although the most successful boy who took the same selection test as me didn't choose to do homework. On reflection, I'm not convinced that homework did me much good – apart from teaching me to work on my own.

Those hoping to attend a grammar school first had to sit a preliminary examination at their junior school to identify whether they were likely to benefit from such an education. If that were the case, on a designated Saturday they had to go to the grammar school and sit at individual desks to take another examination in what seemed to be an enormous hall compared to the one at their junior school.

A schoolmaster or -mistress, dressed in a formal black gown instead of ordinary clothes like the teachers of the junior schools, then gave strict instructions to the candidates that the question paper should not be turned over until permission was given to do so, and then proceeded to walk round the hall putting the papers face down on the desks. After the arithmetic paper (algebra and geometry were not taught then in junior schools) came the English paper, which gave the candidates an opportunity to write a composition. There was also an intelligence quotient test and, because of its design, no one could ever tell how well they had done. For the arithmetic and English exams, however, you would have had a fair idea.

Then came the waiting; had you got through or not? A letter would be sent to your parents and then, arriving home one lunchtime, you would be told the result. If you did very well, you received a scholarship, which meant a free education. If you did *quite* well, you were offered a fee-paying place which would cost your parents £4 a term. Such an offer couldn't be accepted by some children because their parents just couldn't afford the cost. If you went to grammar school, you were expected to stay at least until you'd sat your school certificate examination at 15 years of age, instead of leaving at the age of 14, which was allowed in those days.

But first came your first day at grammar, central or senior school. What a contrast from your junior school! The desks were single and, as you weren't sitting next to anyone, you felt very isolated and cut off; there was no one beside you to whom you could whisper for help and the classes were much smaller, consisting of only about thirty pupils. The school building was larger too. All those corridors and classrooms; would you ever be able to find your way about? And where were the toilets? And some of the boys and girls looked like adults! At junior school you had been the oldest and – most important – trusted enough perhaps to be made a prefect. But here at this new school you were an insignificant nobody!

Junior schools should have warned pupils moving to senior school about the danger of theft. In a junior school, especially a small one, theft was practically unknown, but a senior school, which had more pupils, had a greater likelihood of hiding a thief or two. Senior schools, especially grammar schools, expected pupils to take notes in lessons. This skill should have been taught at junior school, but generally wasn't.

Instead of having the same teacher for all lessons as had been the case at junior school, you had a different teacher for each lesson at senior school. Would I remember their names? And would I remember to call them by their proper name and not their nickname? Some of the subjects were new – what were algebra and geometry? And was chemistry mixing up medicine? Physics sounded as if it was something to do with physical education and goodness knows what we would be taught in biology. Gym and games involved changing into different clothes in front of other children. This was most embarrassing; I'd never had to do that before.

Then there was the gym with its terrifying window ladder. I'd a fear of standing on anything higher than a chair, so how could I possibly have been expected to climb up that dangerous-looking contraption? I didn't like taking risks and so jumping over that leather-covered horse seemed fraught with danger. Then there was this game of 'rugby', which I'd never experienced before. I prided myself on being clean and neat at all times, yet I was expected to throw myself down in the mud and grasp someone's legs; a dirty and most dangerous thing to do which went against everything that I'd been taught earlier.

Moving to a secondary school often meant that you'd miss some of your friends from junior school who would be attending a different one. You probably kept in touch if they lived in the neighbourhood but your interests diverged and you invariably drifted apart, although you might have renewed that friendship later in life.

In the thirties, senior schools were more likely to hold a concert or carol service. Parents' evenings and Parent–Teacher Associations were starting in some schools, but were not very common.

As an indication of how little people travelled from home is shown by the fact that the headmaster of my junior school trained with my paternal grandfather. The school I attended was East Twerton Council School, its initials being ETC, this being said to stand for 'Effort, Tone and Care'. If you produced a particularly good piece of work – an excellent drawing or composition, or pages of ticks in arithmetic – when the headmaster came round, the class teacher put you forward for an ETC, and if the head agreed, he signed his initials. ETCs could also be given for class work such as making a model village that we all helped to build. Teachers were given ETCs, too, for example, for the neat appearance of a classroom. Each week, all the ETCs of a class were added up and, at morning assembly, it was announced which class had won the most.

There were no occasional days off school such as for use as a polling station or for teachers' in-service training. The school attendance officer was efficient at seeing that no one missed school for a frivolous reason. If you were ill in bed, he'd come round and check after a week or so. It was so strict that if you had occasion to visit the school clinic, you were given a card on which the teacher had to write the time you left school. The clinic would insert the time you left it, too, and the teacher noted the time of your return and signed it.

In a village school, a teacher may have been expected to look after three smallish classes comprised of different year groups. One might have been English, another geography, while another might have been busy in the school garden. The infants would probably have had their own teacher, but in order to give them individual attention for reading, they would have been divided into small groups. Others may have been busy modelling with plasticine and learning the rudiments of arithmetic by threading beads. Some schools taught hand weaving on a loom using wool gathered from hedges, deposited by passing sheep. The pupils spun the wool before using it for weaving.

At grammar school, one of my friends devised a wonderful game called 'Fairly Football'. Each time a master used the word 'fairly' meant a goal was scored and, to add to the fun, the masters didn't know that we played one master against another. One particular teacher, nicknamed 'Froggy' because of the harsh tone of his voice, almost never said 'fairly'. Consequently, he never won a match.

Postcard of Chiseldon School, near Swindon, Wiltshire, showing a group of school children dressed for May Day celebrations. (Fred C. Palmer of Tower Studio, Herne Bay, Kent)

It was the custom at that school that, whenever we received a book, we had to write our name, the date of receipt and the book's condition on a label on the inside front cover. This was so that we could be charged if the book was returned with more than ordinary wear and tear. One day, Froggy came in with a pile of textbooks and, as he distributed them, he told us what to write in the 'Condition' column. 'Fairly good. Fairly good,' he chanted as he made his way round the room. We all delighted at the great score he was achieving, although we did our best not to show it. Froggy completely lacked a sense of humour and wouldn't have been at all amused if we'd told him why we were so delighted.

Five

TOWN AND COUNTRY

Town

In the thirties, there were many more independent food shops – grocer's, greengrocer's, fishmonger's, baker's and butcher's – whereas today, supermarkets supply the products these independents used to supply, apart from a very few specialists. There were fewer cafés and cooked-food shops then because, if you were away from home, you took your own food and drink with you; the only takeaways were fish and chip shops. Music shops were more plentiful in those days, selling sheet and bound music, instruments, radios and records. There was often a newsagent and tobacconist in every street and generally a post office within walking distance. Apart from supplying stamps, many people needed postal orders (which children often misheard as 'post lorders') to send with football coupons, for birthday presents, or for the latest fad, a mail order. Home thrift was often practised by both children and adults by depositing money in the Post Office Savings Bank or buying National Savings Certificates. In those days, many shopkeepers lived above their shop or post office.

Almost invariably a stamp machine could be found outside a post office, either fixed to a letter box or on a special stand. Should you have required a stamp when the office was closed, you pushed a halfpenny or penny into a slot and the requisite stamp emerged. One day, when very young, when I tried to tear the stamp off the roll inside the machine, another stamp came out, and then another and another. Not realising that by taking them I was really stealing them, I helped myself to about half a dozen stamps and, although I realised I could have taken a lot more, I thought it would be nice to leave some for the next person to experience the pleasure of free stamps.

Local councils provided more public conveniences – or lavatories – than today because almost none were found in shops. Gentlemen's urinals were free to use, but a penny in the slot was required to gain access to a flushing lavatory.

Most pharmacists, then known as chemists, sold photographic films and accepted exposed ones for developing and printing by an agency, rather than doing it themselves. Many of the medicines they sold, either in liquid or tablet form, were actually made up by them though, relatively few being ready-made.

There being less road traffic, very often you could park outside the shop you were visiting, but as the decade wore on, to avoid congestion, some streets had restricted parking: one side on even dates and the other side on odd dates to make it fair for shopkeepers. There were fewer one-way streets.

There was still quite a lot of horse-drawn traffic, the railway companies particularly favouring this method for town centre deliveries. The horse may have been busily eating with its head in a nose bag, but if it wasn't, it was wise to give its head a wide berth to avoid a nip in case someone had hurt it in the past – perhaps it had learnt that attack was the best form of defence.

A horse and cart were ideal for a milk or bread round because the animal soon learnt where to stop, leaving the milkman or baker to go from house to house, only going to the cart when they needed to top up supplies

Policeman with white armlets directing traffic at a busy intersection. (Author's collection)

in their container or basket. Some goods were moved around the town on two-wheeled push carts propelled by men or lads. Another sight was of sandwich boards worn fore and aft, by a man usually, advertising a product or an event, or perhaps evangelising.

Road repairs were fascinating to watch. One of the first operations was to attach a scarifier (steel hooks) to a steam roller – itself a captivating machine – so that when it moved forwards, it ripped up the old surface to prepare a new road bed. A tar boiler would be lit and the smell that emanated from it was delightful. The liquid tar was then drawn off into a tar pot and poured over the surface, and stones were scattered over it and rolled in. When diesel rollers started to appear later in the decade, it was rather disappointing because they lacked the character of the whistling, puffing, steam variety.

This sort of work often took more than a day, so rather than take the equipment back to the depot, a watchman guarded it overnight. Red-coloured oil lamps were placed around the works, a sentry-like hut placed for the watchman and a brazier, or 'red devil', burning coke placed in front of the hut to keep him warm.

Some roads, instead of being tarred, consisted of wooden blocks. These were fine in the horse transport era providing a quieter surface than tar or stone, but were unsuited to rubber tyres as they made a slippery surface when wet. In the thirties, many councils lifted these blocks and sold them as firewood for which they were well suited as they were impregnated with tar.

Roads and pavements were kept neat and tidy by a road man who came round weekly or fortnightly sweeping by hand with a brush and placing detritus in a hand cart.

Street lighting could be of several varieties. Gas was still very common but had generally been improved by the fitting of a bypass device. This was a very small jet which burnt continuously, but which used very little fuel. It meant that when the gas for the mantle was turned on, it would automatically light. The more up-to-date councils used a clock to turn up the supply to switch the gas on, while others used a cyclist with a long-hooked pole. Lights which were turned on manually offered children the chance to climb the post and turn the gas on so that it would be lit during the daytime.

Electric street lighting could be either by an incandescent bulb like those for domestic use, or if a council was very modern, it would use sodium lighting which gave a better light distribution, especially in foggy conditions, but which made people look unhealthy. These electric lights were operated by a time switch. Some councils adopted helium lights. If your father was thrifty and your bedroom was near a street light, he might insist that you left the curtains open and undressed and dressed by the street light.

Although children of the thirties were no angels, they respected adults and there was almost no vandalism or graffiti. If, therefore, you needed to use a telephone kiosk to make an emergency call, it was not likely to be out of order.

To encourage customers to buy boots and shoes, strings of footwear were hung outside shoe shops. The shop keeper was particularly astute, making sure that only one of a pair, not both, were on display in order to deter theft.

Very nearly all towns, and quite a few large villages, held a cattle market weekly or monthly. Folk from the surrounding area would arrive on market day to do business; trains often had a strengthening carriage to cater for the extra traffic. The railway would also be used for bringing or taking away cattle; road transport for this purpose was little used in this era.

Country

The countryside had a different appearance then: many fields were smaller because farms were not managed on an industrial scale so much; if you were ploughing using a horse, it was not quite so overwhelming ploughing a small field because you realised it wouldn't take too long, whereas if it was a huge field, it would seem to take a lifetime.

Horses had an important role to play on a farm: they were used for carting, ploughing, harrowing and working the elevator. They were labour intensive, having to be fed and groomed, but had the advantage of not compacting the soil as much as a tractor and also, being a living, thinking being, could often help the farmer by anticipating his actions, wants and needs.

Horses were still very useful for hauling felled trees in such steeply graded areas as the Lake District; they also had the advantage of being narrower than a tractor and able to wend their way between several tangled tree trunks.

The hay harvest was an interesting and important event in the days before baling. A few days after the grass had been cut, it was turned with a tedder to make sure it was completely dry. Then a horse rake collected it into long piles. An old cart with wooden rods in front went along a line of piled-up hay and, rather like a bulldozer, pushed it into a heap and then propelled the heap to the rick. Here, the elevator, which was turned by a horse, lifted the hay to the top of the rick where it was spread evenly. The rick was then thatched to render it waterproof. Both children and adults helped with the hay harvest just for the fun of it, not expecting to be paid. When hay was needed in the winter, it was cut from the rick with a large knife.

The corn harvest was equally fascinating. Three main types of cereal were grown in Great Britain: wheat, with its seeds sticking upwards close to the stem; barley, similar to wheat but with a 'beard' to its seed; and lastly oats, with the seeds on long shoots.

First of all, the corn was cut and bound by a horse-drawn machine. Usually, it went round and round the field so the uncut area of corn grew smaller and smaller. This meant that rabbits and other small animals were trapped in the centre and became easy prey to dogs which had been purposely brought to catch them.

The sheaves were placed upright in stooks to dry. When this had been achieved, the sheaves would be collected on a horse-drawn wagon, an elevator used to make a rick which was then thatched.

In due course, a traction engine owned by a contractor drew a threshing machine to the rick yard; as it was only required annually it was not economic for a farmer to buy his own. The binding holding the sheaf was cut and the rest fed into the thresher which separated the seeds from the straw. The thresher was powered by a belt worked off the traction engine.

The potato-harvesting machine avoided the back-breaking job of digging potatoes by hand. The machine consisted of a wheel set at an angle to the ground and raised the spuds so that the boys and men sitting on the machine could pick them up and throw them into sacks.

The author on a horse-drawn hay rake. (G.T. Maggs)

One of the greatest changes to have taken place over the decades in the countryside is the appearance of hedges. Today, hedging all too often means slashing off the tops and sides of a hedge mechanically, leaving it looking like a very amateurish haircut. In the thirties, maintaining a hedge was a work of art and enhanced the look of a field. A stoutish upright main stem of a bush was partly chopped through with a billhook and pushed over to lie parallel with the ground, woven through other uprights. This made a good cattle-proof hedge. The modern slashing method fails to fill any gaps. Hedging and ditching, the latter to ensure good drainage, were winter farming activities.

In the thirties, quite a number of elm trees could be seen in the countryside; a lovely graceful tree, but almost brought to extinction in the 1960s by Dutch elm disease.

Apart from large conurbations like London, milk tended to come from local cows, milked by hand; maybe the farmer himself delivered it. Any unsold milk was converted into butter or cheese by the farmer's wife. She was often also responsible for looking after the hens running about in the farmyard, or confined to a pen, but certainly not a battery.

Country children had plenty of opportunity for fun such as collecting and pressing wild flowers, or collecting birds' eggs; if they were of the larger kind, such as those from moorhens, they would blow them and fry them for breakfast, although these activities are frowned on in these more nature-conscious days. Streams provided many pleasures: paddling, making dams, building bridges, playing Poohsticks and fishing.

Flora and fauna have both suffered since the thirties. Three of the forty-one species of dragonfly, for example, have been lost since that decade and there are fewer lapwings and skylarks to be seen because of changes in farming which affect the varieties of wildflowers. When I was very little, I can remember seeing red squirrels in the trees near my home but by the end of the decade they had all disappeared and been replaced by the far less attractive imported grey squirrels.

In the thirties, there were still many occupation crossings over railways. When they were built, it was quite common for a railway to divide a farmer's land. To accommodate him, therefore, a bridge over the line, or a cattle creep below it, was provided, but if neither were possible, a private level crossing was provided. As it was not protected by signals like a public crossing, it was fraught with danger because the farmer wouldn't know when a train was due and one might have approached when the herd was only partially across.

One landowner was crafty and managed to get his nuts picked free of charge. Living across the road from one of his nut trees, he was able to spot children stealing them. When he estimated that their pockets were nearly full, he crossed the road, accosted them, and then made them hand over all their pickings.

Most villages in the decade had a parish church, post office – probably combined with a shop, school, garage or petrol station, although sometimes the shop sold petrol; frequently there was also a non-conformist chapel.

Six

HOLIDAYS

The four main holidays that parents enjoyed in the thirties were Easter, Whitsun, summer and Christmas.

Good Friday, respecting what was being remembered, was generally a quiet day, a mid-week Sunday in fact. Although a holiday for most workers, curiously, the building trade always worked on Good Friday.

Holy Saturday, or Easter Eve, was a day for gardening, watching spectator sport, or going to the countryside or seaside, the choice depending on whether it was an early or late Easter, for it could be a very cold holiday.

Easter Day involved celebrating the Resurrection of Christ by attending a service in church or chapel, ladies taking the opportunity to show off a new hat or frock.

The opportunities for Easter Monday were much the same as for Easter Eve, before everyone returned to work on the Tuesday.

Whitsuntide, celebrating the coming of the Holy Spirit seven weeks after Easter, has now become rather side-lined. Whit Sunday used to be followed by a bank holiday on Whit Monday, but that was then changed to a late spring bank holiday, which in most years is separate from Whitsuntide. As the weather at Whitsun was likely to be warm, if not hot, it was nevertheless a bank holiday when you could plan to go to the seaside or countryside. Some communities made it an excuse to enjoy a procession.

Summer holidays in the thirties were not for everyone because some couldn't afford to go away and for many it was a week without pay, and it was a week's holiday rather than for a fortnight.

In parts of northern England and the Midlands, it was customary for almost all factories and shops in some towns to close for 'Wakes Week' and they would be virtually deserted as almost everyone would go off to Blackpool.

Something similar happened, too, in the railway town of Swindon. A feature of the GWR works there was the annual 'Trip' during the first week of July. It was held earlier than factories elsewhere in order that locomotives hauling the trains would not be taken from paying passengers at the height of the season a few weeks later.

The Trip had started in 1849 when the GWR treated 500 of its employees to a trip to Oxford by special train. It developed to such an extent that by 1908, no fewer than 24,564 employees and their families in twenty-two special trains were given free travel, most selecting Weymouth as their preferred destination, which became known as 'Swindon-by-the-Sea'. In 1913, the Trip was extended to a whole week and, in 1939, 27,000 left Swindon in thirty special trains. To ease congestion, Trip trains started from various parts of the works, portable steps being provided. Trip week was really a lock out for the workmen until a week's paid holiday was given in 1938, extended to a fortnight ten years later.

Children with prams and four-wheel 'bogies' transported luggage to the station from quite a distance for a couple of pennies while the luggage owners walked as so few buses ran in connection with the Trip trains.

The favourite accommodation away was 'room and attendance' where the trippers would supply food for the landlady to prepare, some families even taking their own vegetables.

If you were particularly short of cash, an inexpensive holiday could be enjoyed by sleeping at home and going by foot, cycle, bus, coach or train on a day trip. This had the advantage that you could choose what to do depending on the weather.

I remember one summer holiday when I discovered a wonderful way of making cash. I found that quite a lot of folk left lemonade bottles on the beach when they left. If I collected them, I could take them to the café and get cash for them. A particularly good time for doing this was in the early evening when most people had gone home and you could clearly see which bottles had been discarded. The only problem was that, by then, the café had closed. Not to be defeated, I dug a large pit in the sand and buried them, very carefully noting a nearby landmark to mark the spot. Next morning, I returned to the beach, dug them up and, when the tide came in, I washed them and deposited them at the café in anticipation of my hard-earned cash. Apparently, I did not wash them very satisfactorily and the café owners asked me to be more careful in future and not get so much sand on them. The income from this source paid for all my ice creams and donkey rides!

Sometimes the rides were led by the donkey owner, or if I was the only rider, the owner would let my father lead me. He was warned that the donkey knew exactly how far it should go before it turned round and that proved to be true. The donkey just obstinately refused to go beyond a certain distance and I was forced to return.

There were also donkeys or ponies drawing four-wheeled carts made into exciting means of transportation such as railway locomotives or aircraft. Riding in one of these you could imagine that you were actually in the real thing.

If you did prefer to holiday away from home, an inexpensive one could be enjoyed by sleeping in youth hostels, but this meant that you were obliged to travel under your own steam – either on foot or cycle. Camping also provided a cheap holiday, while something similar, but more weatherproof, was sleeping in a stationary caravan or grounded old bus which had been converted to living accommodation – which could be seen in many camping and caravan sites.

The author camping at Brean Down near Weston-super-Mare in 1938. His father's Singer car, built in 1930, is in the background and also his mother. (G.T. Maggs)

Another relatively inexpensive holiday was made possible by an innovation introduced by the London and North Eastern Railway (LNER) in July 1933, when it offered holidaymakers the first camping coaches. Ten old carriages had been converted to provide overnight living and cooking facilities and one of these, accommodating six people, could be hired for a week at £2 10s, as long as the holidaymakers travelled by rail. The London, Midland and Scottish Railway (LMS) and the GWR followed suit in 1934 and the Southern Railway in 1935. That year, there were 215 coaches at 162 stations in Great Britain and the figure rose to 439 in 1939. Occupants collected water from the station and were given a key to the toilets and so did not have to pay a penny each time they used them.

Another innovation of the LNER in 1933 was the *Northern Belle* train cruise; the fifteen-coach train provided day and night accommodation for sixty passengers and a staff of twenty-seven. It left King's Cross at 9 p.m. on Saturday and travelled to Barnard Castle. On Sunday, it reached Penrith, where a motor coach took passengers to the Lake District. On subsequent days, the train visited Edinburgh, Aberdeen, Fort William, Mallaig and Craigendoran before arriving back at King's Cross after a week's travel. On three nights out of the seven, the train was stationary and on the other four it was at rest for part of the time. These land cruises were popular and usually fully booked.

On holiday, most people continued to wear their everyday clothes, including a tie, although some might have worn sandals rather than shoes, but would not omit socks. A knotted handkerchief might have been used to keep the sun off your head, particularly if you were bald. Exposed parts of the skin would be treated with calamine solution (a liquid made from zinc carbonate and ferric oxide) to deter damage by the sun's rays.

On the beach, you might sit on one of the corporation's deck chairs, keeping a sharp lookout for the chair attendant who came round with a bag and bundle of tickets rather like a tram conductor. When you spotted him, you might suddenly have realised that there was something you needed to buy urgently in the shops. It was not the custom then to erect windbreaks or use very large sunshades, although some ladies, worried about their complexion, might have held a small umbrella-sized sunshade. Ladies wore a one-piece bathing suit, certainly not a bikini, and men often had a chest covering.

On the beach there was the Punch and Judy Show to watch; perhaps a professionally built sandcastle to admire; there were boat trips out to sea, perhaps trailing a spinner and catching mackerel; then there was the exciting paddle-steamer trip, with the paddles going round and churning up the water. It was exciting and a little frightening going down to a lower deck and seeing the machinery. This type of vessel with its very shallow draught could come surprisingly close to shore. Then there were rafts you could hire to paddle out to sea. This almost proved the end of me when the wash of a Channel Islands steamer swept my father and me off the raft, although my mother managed to stay on.

Weston-super-Mare: Lidos were a popular invention in the 1930s. (Author's collection)

Those who holidayed at home may have had the opportunity to hire a skiff or punt for a trip on the river, or use the river for swimming and fishing. Roller skating was popular in the thirties, but no pads or helmets were worn. The local council provided a slide, swing and roundabout in the local park, but not the variety of activities available today. You could play football or cricket in the park, and if you were lucky, there might have been a funfair or zoo you could attend.

Children, whether rich or poor, generally enjoyed at least one day away if they attended a Sunday school. Most churches and chapels in the thirties ran one. Generally held in the afternoon, they gave parents a chance for peace and quiet while the children enjoyed themselves singing and praying, listening to a story in

Enjoying a picnic. (Courtesy of Stephen Dodds)

small groups and then drawing or acting it. Sometimes special stamps were given for attendance each week; these stamps eventually completed a larger picture when put together. Sunday schools generally held a Christmas party and in the summer provided a free day outing, often to a seaside resort and, for some, this would be the only time they would see the sea that year.

In the thirties, some churches and chapels organised day trips at low prices – made possible because of the large numbers. A tram or bus could be hired to take the party to the station, where they would board a reserved carriage, or perhaps an entire train to take them to the seaside.

Some day trips run by groups during this time could be very adventurous; for instance, a church choir in Bath decided on a trip to Blackpool. When this destination was suggested, the only protest came from the vicar who objected to the choir returning home on the Sabbath, no doubt envisaging a morning service bereft of a choir.

The objection overruled, arrangements were fixed for the trip to take place on Saturday, 11 July 1936, although actually this meant that they left Bath at 11.45 p.m. on Friday. The group arrived at Blackpool North station about 7 a.m. on a grey, cold morning; everyone was then left free to discover their own delights – such as a tram ride to Fleetwood, or the roller coaster at the South Shore.

The return journey from North station left about 12.30 a.m. on the Sunday. Long before it was due to pull out, a very tired group of choristers sat on the station seats listening to an announcement over the public address system. The train before them was destined for Weymouth and one member recalled that the Lancashire pronunciation of West Country place names grated heavily on their West Country ears. Back in Bath every choir member turned up for Matins – but most slept soundly during the sermon!

The build-up to Christmas Day really began towards the end of November on the Sunday before Advent when we heard the collect in the *Book of Common Prayer*:

> Stir up, we beseech thee, O Lord, the wills of thy faithful people; that they, being plenteously bringing forth the fruit of good works, may of thee be plenteously rewarded; through Jesus Christ our Lord. Amen

Hearing this, the ladies in the congregation realised it was time to make the Christmas pudding so that it could mature and be ready for the great day.

The ingredients assembled in a bowl, they would be stirred and then the whole family would stir it some more together and, while stirring, make a wish; children never had a problem deciding what to wish for. The well-mixed ingredients, together with one or two sixpences, were then placed in a basin, covered with greaseproof paper, economically obtained from old butter wrappers, and a piece of cloth was tied over the top. It was then boiled for a whole day, the kitchen being filled with steam the entire time. Following the pudding making, thoughts of Christmas were, to some extent, like the pudding, shelved.

Christmas was less commercialised in the days before the war; shops didn't put up their decorations until early December, while those at home were left until Christmas Eve or just before.

Children in infant and junior classes were given wads of assorted coloured paper strips and some paste on a china palette, and made a section of the hanging chains to run diagonally across the classroom. Each strip was rolled into a circle and pasted to make a link. One lunch time, when the children were out to play, a monitress set out the palettes ready for the first lesson, but – typical of British weather – it started to rain and the children trooped in. One boy felt tempted to touch the paste and then taste it. He thought it tasted good and soon the whole class was consuming the paste. The monitress was horrified, believed they were being poisoned and sped to the staffroom to apprise the teacher of the situation. (It ended well: the children did not die, but the teacher had the trouble of mixing up some more paste.) As schools broke up before Christmas Day, school celebrations had to be a little earlier. Children were told about the true meaning of Christmas; it was about Christ coming into the world and not a time to think about receiving presents and stuffing yourself with food, although the class probably had a party on the last afternoon of term with games such as 'Pass the parcel', 'Musical chairs', 'Blind man's bluff' and 'Pin the tail on the donkey'.

The department stores usually hosted a Christmas grotto and had a post box for letters to Father Christmas.

I remember visiting two such grottos in one afternoon and wondering how Father Christmas managed to get from one to the other without leaving queues of disappointed children. To reach one grotto, we had an 'aeroplane ride' which was extremely exciting when air travel was in its infancy.

Together with my father, I sat on an ordinary chair which had probably been borrowed from the staff rest room; there was no safety belt. After a few moments, a recorded engine noise started and we took off. If you looked down through windows in the floor, a moving strip of paper suggested you were flying over the countryside. I looked through a crack in the side curtain and told my father we were not really moving – but I expect he was well aware of the fact.

Christmas cards were sent much closer to Christmas Day; in fact, there was even a delivery on Christmas morning. One of my father's cousins was thought rather odd because she actually sent cards about two weeks before Christmas – well in advance of the others we received. Owing to financial difficulties, fewer cards were sent than today, usually only being despatched to relatives and close friends whom you wouldn't see on the actual day.

The actual purchase of the cards was much more fun in the thirties. Today you buy them in packs of ten, but back in those days, although a very few boxes of ten or a dozen cards were available, you bought most as single cards, choosing each card with its recipient in mind. This sort of card was more enjoyable to receive because, being priced on the back in pencil, you could look to see how much the sender thought you were worth. Senders who were not too scrupulous were known to carefully alter 2*d* into 5*d*, 3*d* into 8*d* – or make some other amendment.

Mothers were busy in the kitchen, making and decorating the Christmas cake, mince pies and sausage rolls, taking pride in producing good food for their families and certainly not buying it ready-made.

The children were busy decorating the Christmas tree, blowing up balloons and hanging up the decorations.

Fathers arrived home on Christmas Eve at the usual time: no finishing work early in those days. In fact, for some, it meant working longer hours than usual. One particular Christmas, my parents had ordered a toy which was not readily available and the shopkeeper only received it on Christmas Eve, but he took the trouble to deliver it to my parents on his way home at midnight.

The decorations were hung, the Christmas cards arranged on the mantelpiece as they arrived, and coloured lights were draped above the fireplace. When you switched them on, they didn't work, so you tested all the bulbs to find which was the faulty one. Yes, you've guessed correctly, it was always the last one you tested. Not everyone had a Christmas tree; some people couldn't afford one, some didn't have space for one in a crowded room and some mothers who didn't have a vacuum cleaner didn't fancy having to brush up all the needles by hand.

Before children jumped into bed, they remembered to hang up a stocking or pillowcase. Being greedy, I always set out a pillowcase. Getting to sleep was a problem because of the worry as to whether Father Christmas would bring the present you really wanted. Would it be fun to actually see him deliver the presents? Perhaps even talk to him? But sooner or later you'd drift off to sleep. Waking up earlier than usual, you'd feel the stocking or pillowcase. Yes, he really had been, but what had he left?

You either postponed the answer and went back to sleep, or put the light on and investigated. Apart from the big present you hoped for, there were other presents, perhaps something not very exciting like a new pullover, a pair of socks or packet of handkerchiefs. But there would usually also be an apple or orange and some chocolate money covered in gold foil. I wasn't keen on eating raw apples, probably because they weren't always sweet, but I always enjoyed those brought by Father Christmas and told my parents they should buy eating apples from the same place as him, little thinking that, actually, they did!

After dressing in your best clothes on Christmas Day, there was the excitement of playing with the new toys and you probably didn't want to spend much time eating breakfast. Then it was off to church, but no bells at Christmas in 1939 because they had been silenced and were only to be sounded as a signal if the country had been invaded. Mum may not have gone to church but had probably stayed behind to cook the traditional Christmas dinner of chicken or turkey, stuffing, roast potatoes and sprouts, followed by Christmas pudding (will I get the sixpence?), custard and mince pies. This may well have been shared with grandparents or other members of the family, or you may have been invited to their homes to help pull their crackers.

Then being 'FTB' (full to bursting), the afternoon was given over to listening to the King's Speech on the wireless, children having to keep quiet so the grown-ups could listen. As the radio was probably in the only warm room of the house, children were reluctant to leave it and play elsewhere, but as a reward for keeping quiet, after the speech Dad may have lit indoor fireworks. Nuts were popular at Christmas, particularly chestnuts roasted in front of the fire, while walnuts may have been split open with nutcrackers, although I always seemed to find that, as well as crushing the shell, they crushed the walnut inside and there was little of it left to eat.

Afterwards, you might have played cards or a board game before a tea of sandwiches, Christmas cake and more mince pies. In the evening, there would be more games, perhaps spinning the trencher where you sat in a circle and where a wooden plate, or similar object, was spun; the person spinning it then called a name and that person had to reach the spinning plate before it fell over, or pay a forfeit. Another game was passing round a walking stick and tapping it on the floor while chanting, 'You may be very clever but you can't do this', before handing it on anti-clockwise to the next player who probably took it in their right hand, whereas you'd chanted when it was in your left hand.

Then there was 'Squeak piggy, squeak'. You sat in a circle. One person was blindfolded and turned around to ensure they would lose their bearings. They then had to sit on someone's lap and say, 'squeak piggy, squeak'. That person then emitted a curious squeak to disguise who they were but, if identified correctly, it was their turn to be blindfolded.

If you had a piano, it was almost certain to be used as an accompaniment to singing, or you may have listened to gramophone records or the wireless. On Christmas Day, many children were allowed to stay up until midnight, but were very tired and usually fractious by then.

You might have had a lie-in on Boxing Day; certainly Mum and Dad, who'd have gone to bed in the early hours, would have needed one. On Boxing Day morning, you may have visited friends to try out their new presents. Lunch would have been cold meat left over from the day before. In the afternoon, friends or relations may have visited and there would have been more games, or perhaps a visit to the pantomime, often the only opportunity during the year when a child would visit a theatre. Then on 27 December, it was back to work for the adults.

Christmas was less exciting for Scottish children because for nearly 400 years Christmas had been banned there, being considered only a Roman Catholic festival, not to be celebrated by Protestants. It was thus an ordinary working day and it was not until 1958 that it became a holiday in Scotland – just like the rest of Britain. On the other hand, the Scots celebrated Hogmanay with a holiday from 31 December to 2 January when the rest of the country was at work.

Although the blackout had to be observed for Christmas in 1939, it was not all that black outside because it was one of the few occasions when we enjoyed a white Christmas and the snow reflected the light.

At Christmas in 1939, children's toys tended to have a wartime theme: searchlights, planes, Royal Navy ships, guns, tanks, tin helmets and buzzers for practising Morse code.

Seven

TRANSPORT

One great disadvantage of the car today is that you step outside your house, jump into the car, drive off and never meet your neighbours. Children are often driven to school because of all the traffic, quite a proportion of which is other parents driving their children to school! In the thirties, children were rarely driven to school; they generally walked, either alone or with friends, or cycled.

When I was at infant school, my father returned to work following his midday meal just before I had to return for afternoon school so he gave me a lift on his bicycle, purchasing a small saddle which he fixed to the crossbar, my feet being placed in stirrups. On another occasion, one morning when walking to school, the friend who usually accompanied me came along in a horse and cart and offered me a lift.

Horses were still popular and economic when used for short journeys. As mentioned earlier, they were ideal for milk and bread rounds. The railway companies still used large numbers for various purposes: delivering goods in towns and shunting wagons and coaches if no locomotive was available.

I lived on quite a steep hill and before descending with the horse-drawn dust cart, the driver would place a skid, some called it a 'slipper', under one of the rear wheels. This was a length of cast iron on to which a wheel would be run to stop it rotating; the friction of the skid on the road would prevent the cart from overcoming the horse and plunging downhill.

Once a week the rag-and-bone man would come round with his horse and cart. He literally terrified me. His exceedingly loud voice frightened me when I was a small boy and if I was in the front garden when he came, I sped to the back.

Most people lived within approximately 2 miles of a station, which meant that if you wanted to collect or deliver anything, the horse and cart didn't have to travel further than 2 miles; it also meant that if you had to go there yourself on foot it was an acceptable distance and could be reached in about half an hour.

When I was very young, the city in which I lived still had an electric tramway system. Younger people referred to the vehicles as 'trams' while older folk called them 'cars', although the terms varied in different parts of the country.

The tramcars themselves were fascinating to a young boy. In my city, they were repainted every two years and kept in splendid condition; in fact that was one of their drawbacks, they were built so well and lasted so long that their design – open tops and wooden seats harking back to the outside seats of stage coaches – were outdated before they wore out and passengers pressed for enclosed motor buses with upholstered seats.

Open-top trams were much more romantic than closed-in buses. One lad I knew, when he sat on the top deck of the tram, liked to lean over the side and spit down on an attractive girl as she boarded. He eventually married her and they lived happily ever after – well for fifty-six years any rate.

Double-deck open-top trams and buses were fitted with 'modesty boards'. Often covered with an advertisement, these were fixed to the tram and bus sides to shield women's and girls' legs and ankles from the view of those on the street.

The tramway system I knew as a boy was single track with passing loops. To avoid drivers having to alter the points set every quarter mile or so apart, they were permanently set for the left-hand track and, when a tram reached the far end of the loop, they forced open the point blade which was set for a tram going in the opposite direction. This action caused the sound 'tin-top, tin-top' as the two sets of wheels on the four-wheeled trams forced the blade open. Nobody ever explained this to me at the time and it was years later and well after the tramway had been lifted that I discovered the reason for the sound. I was always disappointed that my O gauge model tram going over my Hornby points didn't also sound the satisfying 'tin-top, tin-top'. I now know why.

But the open-tops were fun. You could twist a tram ticket into a propeller shape, thrust it through a pin and lean with it over the side of the top deck and, if you had designed it correctly, see it spin round as the tram went along. Downstairs you could sit behind the front glass doors and actually watch the motorman at the controls.

The motorman controlled two pedals – one for the gong and the other for sand, this one being necessary for starting or stopping if the rail was greasy. He also operated two handles: one to control the power and magnetic brake; the other the reversing handle. In addition, he had to operate the handbrake.

Trams were very safe because, as well as the handbrake, a driver could use the magnetic brake which turned the motors into generators to magnetise a brake shoe pressing on the rail. The faster a tram travelled, the more electricity would be generated and thus the more powerful the magnet became, bringing the tram to a halt quicker.

A further safety feature was the lifeguard tray. At the front of the tram, below the driver's platform, were two or three horizontal bars known as the lifeguard gate. In the event that something came into contact with the gate – a dog perhaps, or even a person – the gate would automatically retract, causing the lifeguard tray to descend and scoop up whatever had struck the gate before it was crushed by the wheels!

In addition to the handbrake and magnetic brake, some trams also had an air brake and, if all braking systems failed, the driver could always put the motors into reverse.

A further safeguard was that, before a tramway system could be opened, it had to be inspected by the Board of Trade. It was essential that a Board of Trade stop be placed at the top of each steep incline and a tram halted at these stops whether or not a passenger wished to get on or off. This ensured that the tram was under control before its descent.

Initially, as a child when playing at being a tram driver, I used the handle of a casement window as a controller handle, but then as the railed steps outside my back door were not

This small boy doesn't look happy at leaving this Bath electric tram, or was it because he didn't like being photographed? (Author's collection)

unlike a tram driver's platform, my father converted two old walking sticks into a controller handle and handbrake.

In the thirties, drivers and conductors wore smart uniforms and polished black boots. If their boots weren't black, they were sent home without pay for that day. A conductor wore a leather money bag over one shoulder, a bell ticket punch on a strap over the other shoulder and a whistle for signalling to the driver when they weren't near a bell, although sometimes they stamped hard on the floor, or banged their ticket rack against the side of the tram – quick and clever ways to alert the driver, albeit unofficial.

A boy's birthday or Christmas present in the thirties often consisted of a tram conductor's set which comprised a bell punch, money bag, whistle, ticket rack and cap. When everyone was aboard, the bus or tram conductor (in some towns called a 'guard'), called out, 'Hold tight please' and rang the bell twice to inform the driver that it was safe to move on. If the vehicle had its full complement of passengers, they would sound three rings to the driver who would then not stop unless someone wished to get off. When all the fares were collected, the conductor was required to stand – not lean – on the rear platform. Some inspectors checked conductors' uniforms – if they had a sheen, it meant the conductors had been leaning!

Some seaside tramways had open-sided trams, either roofed or completely open, and were known as 'toast racks' because that's precisely what they looked like. The

conductor on these collected fares while climbing along
the running board. Some tramways had single-deck
'combination' cars which offered passengers a choice
of either travelling in the enclosed centre saloon, or at
one of the ends, which although roofed and with sides,
were open at the end. If you smoked, you had no choice
where to sit as these were specially designated seating
areas for smokers. Passengers sat immediately behind the
driver who had to be careful that if a road user caused
them to brake sharply, they were to be sure not to use an
expletive to offend delicate ears.

Some systems used a bell punch and coloured tickets
for different price denominations, while others used a
'hurdy-gurdy'. The conductor dialled the price and then
turned a handle which triggered a ticket to be printed
on a strip of white paper. I far preferred the coloured
ticket system.

The coloured tickets were numbered and, when the
conductor came on duty, they were required to note
the first number denomination and note it again when
they'd finished their turn so that the value of the tickets
they'd sold would equal the cash in their bag. As a further
check, each time the bell punch was operated, a counter
moved, so the number of punches should have equalled
the number of tickets. If there was any dispute over the
number, as the punch stamped out a portion of the ticket,
just like confetti, these small pieces could be counted.

Nearly all of the first-generation British trams were
double-deck and double-ended. This meant that at

the end of a trip, the driver would lift the two control handles and walk to the other end of the car. The rear then became the front. Meanwhile, the conductor had swung the backs of the lateral seats so that passengers would face the new direction of travel. The trolley pole which collected the current from the overhead wire also had to be swung round. When the arm was pulled down, the electricity supply would be disconnected and the tram lights thus switched off. This posed no problem if there was street lighting, but if there was none, the conductor had to feel for the relatively thin wire in the dark.

As money was short, people took great pains to save even a halfpenny. If your destination was just a stop beyond a fare stage, rather than pay the extra, many people would walk the extra distance.

Trams were so well made then that they lasted for years. In fact, in Bristol those trams built in the 1890s were still running in 1940. This meant that their design was out of date: the open tops of double-deck trams – which most British trams were – were fine on a hot summer's day, but left something to be desired in a blizzard. The modern motor bus, even though it lacked heating in the thirties, was much cosier.

The answer seemed to be the electric double-deck trolleybus, but time proved otherwise. They were roofed and had upholstered seats and ran almost silently, but there were nevertheless disadvantages. Their silence meant that it was all too easy to step off the pavement in front of one. When they replaced a tramway system, two wires, rather than one, were needed to collect power (there was no rail for the return), and the standards used for supporting tram wires were not strong enough and needed to be replaced. As a trolleybus was single ended, it meant that at a terminus a turning circle was required which was either, literally, a circle to run round, or a square of streets. At Christchurch neither was available. The solution was to run the trolleybus on a turntable and the driver and conductor had to push it round 180 degrees. Like a tram, its route was fixed, and thus if a road needed to be temporarily closed, there was no possibility of diversion. The trolleybus used more power than a tram because running on rubber tyres created more friction than steel wheels on steel rails. Thus, in due course, trolleybuses disappeared from British streets, but trams have made a comeback, now with state-of-the-art design and technology.

At this time, motor buses were propelled by two forms of internal combustion engine. The majority had petrol engines, but diesel engines using a cheaper fuel were becoming popular and had become dominant by the end of the decade. Double-deck buses at the time were mainly for urban use and tended not to be seen outside in rural communities, which were chiefly served by single-deckers.

Most buses of the era were of the forward-control design where the driver sat alongside the engine, while at the rear was an open platform for passengers to board. The conductor stood here when they were not collecting fares. Drivers and conductors were almost invariably men; driving was hard work with unassisted steering and a heavy gear box. Most seats faced the direction of travel, but those over the rear wheels faced each other on opposite sides of the bus.

As some bus routes ran in competition, the railways took over the control of some bus companies: the Southern Railway was associated with Southern National; GWR with Western National; and the LNER with Eastern National.

An important date for travellers in the London area was 13 April 1933 when an Act was passed to set up the London Passenger Transport Board (LPTB) to provide a co-ordinated transport system for all rail and road transport in partnership with the mainline railways which continued to retain control of their London suburban services. The LPTB covered an area of 1,986 square miles and took over five railway companies, fourteen municipal tramways, three private tramway companies and sixty-one bus companies. In 1934, the LPTB owned 174 route miles of railway, 3,072 electric cars, 84 locomotive-hauled coaches, 51 electric and 38 steam locomotives. Despite its name, it did not just deal with passengers. In 1934, it also handled 3 million tons of goods and coal and 56,000 head of cattle. The formation of the LPTB was not entirely welcomed by transport enthusiasts as it meant the loss of many liveries and the onset of standardisation.

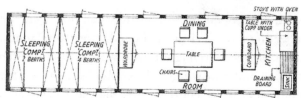

Plan of Great Western camping coach

Plan of a GWR camp coach for six holidaymakers.

In the thirties, the best way to travel a significant distance in Britain was to go by train. In pre-motorway
days, travel along snake-like roads was slow, especially if
the road was narrow and it was difficult to overtake a
heavy commercial vehicle whose speed was limited by
law to 20mph. Although road coach travel was cheap, it
too was slow.

Coaches of the thirties were of forward-control
design like a bus, but instead of an open platform, they
had a door either at the front or rear. The roof could be
slid open for ventilation and there was a ladder at the
rear for the driver to climb when they were stacking
luggage on the rear part of the roof.

When on holiday in Weymouth in the mid-thirties,
I remember pleading for a ride on a very unusual bus
which ran to Bowleaze Cove. Made by Shelvoke &
Drewry Limited of Letchworth, Hertfordshire, it had
a 14 horse-power engine with three forward gears and
Ackerman steering. Its sides were open and the conductor in a white smock climbed along the running board

to collect fares. It had unusually small wheels, as did the dustcarts made by the same firm. Similar buses could also be found in Worthing.

Arguably, steam railways reached their prime in the thirties and their development excited children. The decade, however, could have begun with a serious accident.

On 23 January 1930, as the up *Golden Arrow* was approaching Kent House station, the leading and centre coupled wheels of the locomotive derailed. Luckily, the middle wheels soon rerailed themselves, but the leading set ran 880 yards before getting back on to the track. Curiously, the crew was quite unaware of what had happened and the incident was only discovered when damage to the permanent way was detected. It nevertheless arrived at Victoria on time.

The decade was marked by the increase of speed. In September 1931, the GWR cut the time of the Cheltenham Flyer to 67 minutes for the 77.3 miles between Swindon and Paddington, thus achieving an average speed of 69mph. On 5 June 1932, the distance was covered at an average speed of 81mph.

1931 saw the innovation of a petrol road–rail vehicle built by Karrier for the LMS. It was a twenty-two-seater bus capable of running on either road or rail. Flanged wheels were fitted to the axles and on the outside of these were pneumatic-tyred road wheels.

The LMS had opened the luxury Welcome Hotel at Stratford-upon-Avon and from 23 April 1932, Shakespeare's birthday, until 2 July 1932, this road–railer ran from the hotel to the station and then onwards by rail to Blisworth, where passengers could change to a London train. Although otherwise successful, it proved too heavy and was withdrawn following the breakage of a front axle.

1932 marked the beginning of the end of the steam locomotive in Britain, for that year the LMS bought a diesel–electric shunter which became the prototype for future designs.

Early in 1932, a Micheline railcar was tested by the LMS between Bletchley and Oxford: the first rail vehicle in Britain to use pneumatic tyres. A gauge on each wheel monitored the air pressure and if it fell to in excess of 14 pounds per square inch below the normal pressure of 85 pounds per square inch, an audible warning sounded. A spare wheel carried on board could be fitted in about five minutes. The LMS authorities disliked its almost silent operation and thus did not adopt it.

In 1933, Hardy Motors Limited built a streamlined diesel railcar seating sixty-nine passengers. Driven by a standard 130 horse-power bus engine, it was capable of a maximum speed of 60mph. Bought for £3,249 by the GWR, its successors formed the basis for British Railways' diesel units built twenty-five years later.

In 1935, Nigel Gresley, the LNER's locomotive engineer, felt that at speeds of over 70mph, streamlining would reduce air resistance and so modified his express locomotive design to haul a new train, the *Silver Jubilee*. To further reduce air resistance, the gangway connections between the seven coaches were full width; engine and train were finished appropriately in silver grey with stainless-steel lettering. Twice during its first run it reached a maximum of 112½mph, achieving a railway record.

Locomotive spotters were excited in 1935 by a new type of steam engine driven by a turbine, rather than pistons. It proved efficient and marginally more frugal in water and coal consumption and it offered smoother running, but its main drawback was that, being a one-off, spare parts were not readily available, so was periodically out of service waiting for them.

An excitement for young railway enthusiasts on 14 October 1936 was the sleeper service inaugurated between London and Paris. A train ferry could carry either twelve sleeping cars or forty goods wagons spread over four tracks. The trains left Victoria and the Gare du Nord each night at 10 p.m. and 9.50 p.m. respectively, the corresponding arrivals being 8.55 a.m. and 8.30 a.m.

The aim was not to produce a fast service, but a comfortable one, allowing a passenger to go to bed on leaving Victoria and wake up in France in time to dress and have breakfast on the train before reaching Paris. As the coaches had to be chained to the ferry deck and then unchained on the other side of the Channel, passengers didn't enjoy an entirely undisturbed rest. On board, they were locked in the sleeping cars and this could have been dangerous had the ship struck a rock or another vessel. As the lavatories at the end of the cars discharged their waste straight on to the track, on the ferry, sump boards were placed in strategic positions to collect it.

In 1937, the London, Midland and Scottish Railway inaugurated the
Coronation Scot train, seen here headed by the streamlined locomotive
Coronation. (Author's collection)

The carriage compartments of the night ferry were
unlike most others as they contained a sickness bowl
(*vase de nuit*), a lifebelt and a net for securing luggage.
The *vase de nuit* often had an alternative use! The class of
passenger using that service later defected to air travel.
The last night ferry ran on 1 October 1980.

The LMS, not to be outdone by Gresley's *Silver Jubilee*,
also produced a streamlined engine and on 29 June 1937
showed it off by running a press trip from London to
Crewe and back, achieving a record speed of 114mph.
Unlike the LNER, its train did not comprise specially
built coaches, but was ordinary stock, painted in a distinctive livery. From the horse-drawn delivery wagons
in the yard to the modern streamlined locomotives at

the platform, the railways of the period certainly offered a vast range of contrasts.

The GWR directors, feeling that they must acknowledge the trend for streamlining, persuaded their reluctant locomotive engineer to streamline two of their engines. This was achieved by smoothing plasticine over a model and the result was as unpleasant as you would expect it to be. Within a few years, all the superficial additions had been removed from the two engines.

On 3 July 1938, the LNER's *Mallard* (named after Gresley's favourite bird at his moated home near St Albans) achieved a speed of 126mph, a record unlikely to ever be surpassed by steam.

The decade saw the declining years of a very useful type of locomotive which had been in use for about eighty years. This was the six-wheeled engine, technically known as a 0-6-0. As all its weight was on its driving wheels, it was very sure-footed. Although normally intended for goods traffic, it was also suitable for hauling long but slowish passenger trains, such as those used for cheap excursions. Being so adaptable, it could haul freight trains from Monday to Friday and then a passenger train on Saturday when more trains had to be available because holidaymakers almost invariably travelled on Saturdays. All four mainline railways owned many locomotives of this type.

One railway vehicle which became defunct in 1935 was the steam railmotor, which had been an entirely new concept when it first appeared in 1903. At the start of the twentieth century, electric tramways were being laid down in many towns and these were serious competition to urban railways as tramways had more frequent stops and were generally located closer to passengers' homes. A railmotor was really a combined locomotive and passenger coach on the same underframe. The fireman stayed at the boiler end, but as the driver could drive from either end, it saved the time and trouble of having to run a locomotive round at the end of each journey and so was particularly useful when operating short journeys. Lateral seats were usually hinged so that they could be swung over to face the direction of travel.

When a railmotor service was introduced, 'halts' – as unstaffed platforms were called – were established so as to offer an increased number of stops and thus make the service more accessible. Fares were collected tramway-style by a conductor who doubled as a guard. Over time, problems were found in the railmotors: the passenger saloon became dirty when resting in a locomotive shed; the passenger end lay idle while the locomotive section was being serviced. They were eventually replaced by small locomotives whose trains could be pulled and pushed.

In the late 1920s, the LMS and the LNER introduced Sentinel railcars of lighter construction than a railmotor, driven by the type of engine used in a steam lorry. They were withdrawn between 1935 and 1948.

Contemporary with the Sentinels, Clayton Wagons Limited constructed similar cars which were also bought by the LNER. They had a short life, however, the last being withdrawn in 1937.

The last Sentinel railcar to enter service on a British railway was a rail bus, specially designed for the Southern Railway's steeply graded Brighton to Dyke branch. Extraordinarily light, it only weighed 17 tons 4 hundredweight. The wheels were fitted with external drum brakes with road-pattern brake shoes inside. Supplies of coal and feed water were automatic so the car could be manned by just a driver. Entering service on 1 May 1933, it was fast, economical and comfortable. On test, its acceleration was phenomenal, achieving a maximum of 61mph and consuming 4.99lb of coal per mile. When overloaded in 1935, its frame broke and after repair it was transferred to the Westerham branch before being withdrawn in 1936.

Some of the constituent companies forming the Southern Railway in 1923 had introduced electric tram in the London area. In his 1929 budget, the Chancellor of the Exchequer announced that the railway passenger duty levied on first- and second-class fares would be abolished – on condition that the railway companies spent the capitalised value of the duty in improvement and development schemes to relieve unemployment.

Supplementary ticket for journey in a GWR Birmingham to Cardiff streamlined diesel railcar.

The Southern Railway decided to use the offer to electrify lines to Brighton and Worthing and the electrified line to Brighton was opened on 30 December 1932; the electrified line to Hastings via Eastbourne on 4 July 1936; and to Portsmouth on 4 July 1937. Thus, by 1939 the Southern had the world's largest suburban electric network.

The decade witnessed the twilight of an appealing form of transport – the light railway. Unless a railway company owned the land on which it wished to build a line, an Act of Parliament was required in order to gain powers of compulsory purchase. Such an Act was expensive to obtain, yet some areas of Great Britain needed a railway although it would hardly be economic. Less expensive lines needed to be set up and needed to be cheaper to operate.

The solution was to be found in the Light Railways Act which had been introduced much earlier in 1896 and allowed the light railway commissioners to grant a light railway order for it to be built. Local authorities were permitted to make loans for such a purpose and, when the line was finished, it could be operated more cheaply. Cattle grids were introduced instead of manned level crossings with gates; stations were no longer required to be staffed; simpler signalling arrangements were introduced – but all at the expense of a low speed limit.

Unfortunately, at just about the same time a light railway opened, motor buses were introduced and their routes were in direct competition with the light railway, able to collect passengers nearer to their homes and deliver them closer to their destinations at a cheaper price and just as quickly. Many light railways, therefore, only enjoyed a lifetime of about thirty years.

What was fascinating about these light railways was their equipment, which was often old third- or fourth-hand equipment from another railway – perhaps coaches with open-ended verandas so that you could stand out-side and pretend you were in the Wild West. Sometimes, in an effort to run them economically, very modern features were added, such as petrol-driven railcars – one carried spare cans of petrol with their caps missing alongside the passengers. Fordson tractors, adapted for rail work, were used for shunting. All these fascinating things disappeared with the light railways.

In the thirties, those employees in the public eye were often seen sporting smart uniforms, whether they were in charge of the various forms of transport, delivered the post, were employed by the waterworks, in the cinemas or worked as lift attendants (lifts were not self-service at the time). A smart uniform was something an employee could be proud of and also showed respect to the public – because customers were considered very important. In the thirties, if you wore the wrong uniform, such as brown rather than black shoes or boots, then you were sent home and forfeited a day's pay.

By the end of the decade, most of the larger commer-cial vehicles had their diesel engines in the cab with the driver sitting alongside in order to maximise space for payload. It was at this time that heavy lorries and buses changed from petrol to diesel engines, although lighter commercial vehicles and cars still favoured petrol. They all had pneumatic rather than solid tyres.

Children seemed to find the steam lorry particularly interesting. With a flat, sloping front, very similar to today's express trains, the cab contained a vertical coke-fired boiler. Compared with the contemporary diesel engine, they were quiet and fast, particularly uphill. I thought they left a very pleasant smell behind, although my mother disagreed.

As a young child, I called these delightful vehicles 'motor lorry puffers' which described them admirably. I was told sternly by my father, however, that the proper name was 'steam lorry' which I didn't think described them half as well. At the time, there were three types of propulsion for lorries: horse, steam and motor.

As I mentioned earlier, I lived on quite a steep hill – and still do – and just outside my home, very heavily laden lorries would have to change into a lower gear. Bedford lorries in particular emitted an exceptionally unpleasant shriek in bottom gear and, if I was driving my pedal Vauxhall by the front gate, I would pedal away like mad to escape from it. I was even more terrified by these lorries when a driver made a hash of changing gear and the vehicle started to roll backwards. As the bottom gear had no synchromesh (a mechanism involved in gear changing), double de-clutching was essential to ensure a smooth change.

A preserved Sentinel steam lorry in the yard at Midsomer Norton station. (Author's collection)

The author in charge of a horse brake at Upwey following a trip from Weymouth in 1935. (G.T. Maggs)

The chain-driven, 2-stroke Trojan was quite a different vehicle in terms of its appearance and the sound it emitted. Brooke Bond Tea – one of the nation's favourite brands of tea – favoured this particular make of van. Another unusual vehicle which attracted me was the three-wheeled delivery van with a front like a motor bike and the rear like an ordinary van. I was always disappointed that there was never any commercial model equivalent made and was not sufficiently skilled with my hands to scratch-build one.

In the thirties, there was still a great variety of cars for youngsters to look out for; the majority were British built, foreign makes being rare. In that era, cars were used for both business and pleasure, but not usually for travelling to or from work. It was a decade of chromium and shiny things, which particularly appealed to children; chromium could be seen on cars, shop fronts and household articles.

In the dark, a skilled ear could identify the make of an approaching car by its distinctive sound. Three-wheeled cars were particularly attractive because they just seemed so different. The Morgan with its single wheel at the rear was also distinctive as was the BSA with its wheel at the front. It was generally believed that it was easier to overturn a BSA than a Morgan as the Morgan had a wider track and was thus more stable. The 2-stroke Jowett had its own characteristics and its handbook stated that all Jowett owners were friends and should wave to each other when passing.

It was only at the end of the thirties that cars were given boots, and for economy reasons, some cars only had access to the boot from *inside* the car. Until then, luggage was secured on a carrier at the back, while the spare wheel was also fixed at the back or on the running board. There were no dipping mirrors, and thus a blind operated by a long cord could be drawn by the driver over the rear window to avoid dazzle. There were no heaters or demisters, but to clear a windscreen of mist, or keep a car cool in summer, you could open the front windscreen. Many cars had sliding roofs, but they tended to leak. Only one rear lamp was required, but at night, side lights had to be illuminated when a car was parked on the street. Consequently few people left their cars on the road overnight and instead used garages. The drum brakes used tended to fade on long, steep hills, so a wise motorist descended in low gear.

Sometimes it was a nuisance driving uphill. Some cars, such as Fords, had windscreen wipers which worked by suction from the inlet valve so when the engine was pulling hard, you had to ease off the accelerator to get the blades to move. Most cars only had a wiper for the driver's side. Car radios were rare because you were required to purchase another radio licence in addition to the one for your home.

The springs in Fords were placed laterally so that one spring served two wheels instead of having a spring for each wheel. This proved quite economical. Standards also had this system on the front axle. Trafficators (or indicators) were becoming common, but as they tended to be unreliable, and didn't protrude or go back in when they were supposed to, hand signals were still widely used to indicate a driver's intention to turn.

Motor bikes were British built and of the 2- or 4-stroke variety. Those who couldn't afford a car could sometimes manage to run a motor bike and sidecar, the initial expense, running costs and road tax all being cheaper than those for a car.

As traffic was increasing on the roads, the Minister of Transport, Hore Belisha, became more and more concerned over the number of road fatalities. One solution was the introduction of 'Belisha crossings' where pedestrians were given priority over vehicles.

One of my cousins was told that at these crossings, the driver *had* to stop, so he thought he would carry out a test. He ran over a crossing immediately in front of a car, failing to give the driver an opportunity to stop. He was knocked over! Fortunately, he was not seriously injured.

That particular cousin of mine lacked road sense. A cyclist, he discovered that if he rode close behind a bus, its slipstream would ease his progress. What he failed to foresee was that he was riding so close to the bus that if it stopped suddenly he would run into its rear. The inevitable did happen, and again my cousin ended up in hospital.

At busy road junctions, police officers wearing white armlets stood on point duty. At dangerous junctions where there were no officers, an AA or RAC officer, equipped with white armlets, would perform this duty as a public service to all road users, not just to members of the organisation.

Another safety device in the thirties was traffic lights at dangerous junctions to avoid the need for police officers to be on point duty. Initially, these lights were time-operated, but fairly frequently a vehicle had to wait when nothing was coming the other way, so pads were placed in the road to detect when a vehicle was approaching. This, however, was not without its problems. When riding my horse, it carefully stepped *over* the pads (rather than *on* them) and if nothing was following me, I had to dismount and jump on them myself in order to activate them.

Electric trams faced the same problem, but the driver did not need to stop and get out. A switch was fitted to the overhead wire and when the trolley passed this particular contact, it had the same effect as the rubber pad.

In those days, councils dealt with icy roads by sending out a lorry with staff in the back to shovel out grit. Their trajectory only managed to reach the road, leaving the pavements untouched. Today, with the very efficient mechanical gritters in operation, pavements can be sprayed as well as the road. In reality though, the pavements are often still not gritted because of the parked cars which hamper the operation.

One innovative feature of the decade was the use of battery-powered vehicles for the daily delivery of milk and bread. These vehicles made a gentle purr. In some towns, merchants used them for coal delivery. The great

Road signs introduced in the 1930s.

advantage of these vehicles was that, when making frequent stops, you didn't need to keep starting the engine, an important consideration in the days of weak batteries. As weak batteries were so likely, carrying a starting handle was essential so that the engine could be manually turned. This operation wouldn't have been practical on a bread round though.

It is notable how Remembrance Day was commemorated each 11 November. At 11 a.m., there was a two-minute silence. Road traffic stopped and drivers stepped out and stood to attention, while trains came to a halt at a station or signal box.

Similar to a steam roller but with ordinary wheels fitted with solid rubber tyres, was the traction engine which was capable of hauling trailers with various loads, or wheeled farm machinery for threshing. By the thirties, roads had almost said farewell to these delightful vehicles, which by then were only used by owners of fairground rides who hauled them around the countryside and which powered the electric generator when the fairs were set up.

Every few miles along a road, a blacksmith and a farrier – one who specialised in shoeing horses – could be found. The smithy could provide hours of entertainment: you watched the iron being placed in the fire, then being taken out red or white hot, being shaped and then being plunged into a tank of cold water where it hissed.

Then there were the horses themselves who may or may not have been co-operative and lifted a leg. There was the placing of the hot shoe on the hoof to be burnt in – all great fun to watch, especially when on one particular day, I saw my horse's hoof go up in flames! I was scared that his whole coat would catch alight! But my horse remained calm and had every faith in the farrier, who quickly doused the blaze.

The 1930s was a decade when horse transport in town and country was being replaced by the mechanical variety; some blacksmiths changed to being motor mechanics, turning smithies into garages. Most garages were not tied to selling one particular brand of petrol, but sold a wide variety. Some pumps were operated electrically; the volume of petrol being delivered was indicated by a clock-like hand on a dial marked in gallons. You therefore ordered by the gallon, not price. You were *served* with petrol – you did not help yourself. The attendant frequently cleaned the windscreen and offered to check the engine's oil level too.

Other pumps were worked by hand and their operation was fascinating to watch. The attendant would place the hose in the vehicle's tank and then rock a handle backwards and forwards to pump the petrol up into a glass tank at the top of the column. When the required amount had been pumped, the attendant would open a valve and the petrol would flow down into the vehicle's tank; the attendant would conclude the operation by lifting the hose to make sure every drop of petrol had run into the tank. Cars of the period consumed quite a lot of oil, and thus an oil cabinet was a feature of a garage forecourt.

Many adults rode a bike and it was an impressive sight to stand outside a large works and see swarms of cycles coming out at the end of a shift. As many workers went home for their dinner (lunch) hour, this speedy method of travel was essential to ensure it could be done in the time available. Children longed for a bike but quite often parents just couldn't afford one. When it was dark, a lamp had to be fixed to the front of bicycles. Most were lit by batteries at that time but there were still some carbide ones around, left over from an earlier period. For those to function, water was dripped on to carbide to make a gas which was then lit. This involved a lot more fuss than just switching on a battery. No rear lamp was required, just a white patch on the bottom of the rear mudguard and a red reflector. If you really wanted to be up to date, you had a dynamo which generated current by a wheel rubbing against the wall of a tyre. Most bikes were single gear, but if you had the money, you could buy a Sturmey-Archer 3-speed, or a derailleur. My next-door neighbour had a battery-operated warning horn on his bike which I enjoyed sounding as I could reach over the wall and blow it from my front path. It emitted a less penetrating sound than a bell though, and a bell needed no battery, a great advantage when money was short. An interesting cycle accessory was a mileometer so that you could tell how far you'd travelled. There was also a speedometer available but my father rightly said that he'd never let me have one of these as it would encourage me to go too fast.

In the thirties, there was still a significant number of barges and narrow boats on British waterways, some still horse drawn. As 1930s children travelled far less than today's, many not exploring far beyond their street, town or village, the majority of inland children would never have seen large ocean liners. In fact, many wouldn't even have seen a skiff or narrow boat on a canal or river.

Those living in ports would have been impressed by ocean liners operated by such companies as Cunard and P&O, carrying passengers and mail to far-off places; air travel was not really available to general members of the public and was very much reserved for the future. To speed up mail and a few impatient passengers, tenders set out from Plymouth to meet incoming vessels bound for Southampton and the mail was transferred to them. A special train sped to London, arriving well before the other passengers had disembarked at Southampton.

At this time, there were fleets of estuary and coastal paddle steamers which some children would have seen and perhaps travelled on if their parents were sufficiently affluent. There were many of these vessels on the Clyde; they were used by commuters to travel to work and also by day trippers for pleasure. The steamers on the Thames and Severn estuaries and those serving various coastal resorts were solely for people's enjoyment.

Paddle steamers were exciting. You could watch the paddles rotating and churning up foam and when on board, there was the thrill of descending to the engine room, the smell of the oil and the sight of the large, shining and thumping machinery turning the paddles.

Domestic air travel was introduced during this decade, initiated by the railways, realising that it was the latest challenge to their monopoly of transport. They could not have established it without an Act of Parliament which was secured by the Big Four: GWR, LNER, LMS and the Southern Railway. GWR was the first to make use of these powers and, on 12 April 1933, opened a service between Cardiff, Haldon (sited just inland from Dawlish and serving Teignmouth and Torquay) and Plymouth.

The plane, a three-engine, six-seater Westland Wessex, built appropriately in GWR territory at Yeovil, was painted in a chocolate and cream livery like the company's passenger coaches, and its interior décor was similar to that of a standard first-class railway compartment. Imperial Airways supplied the plane, pilot and ground staff for the twice-daily flights. It took about 50 minutes to cover the 80 miles, compared with almost 4 hours and 140 miles by rail which could not cut directly across

the Bristol Channel. Initially, the single fare from Cardiff to Plymouth was a very expensive: £3 10s, or a return could be purchased for £6. The railway provided buses to connect with Cardiff General, Torquay and

Enjoying a day out on a train!
(Courtesy of Stephen Dodds)

Plymouth North Road stations and also the enquiry bureau at Teignmouth town hall. On 22 May 1933, the service was extended to Birmingham.

From 15 May 1933, the railway received permission from the postmaster general to carry mail on this service. A special GWR airmail stamp, costing threepence, had to be fixed in addition to the ordinary three halfpence General Post Office stamp. When the seasonal service ended on 30 September 1933, only 714 passengers had been carried by air and the operation had cost the company £6,526.

In 1934, the Big Four, in association with Imperial Airways, formed the Railway Air Services Limited, but flights ceased at the outbreak of war in 1939. In 1944, the Big Four published a plan for the development of air transport to Europe, but a change of government in 1945 brought an end to railway involvement in air transport and British European Airways took over the railway airlines on 1 April 1947. It was not until the Railways Act of 1993, however, that the 1929 air powers were extinguished.

Eight

THE ONSET OF THE SECOND WORLD WAR

The Spanish Civil War (1936–39) had shown that a new aspect of hostilities was aerial bombing. With the rise of Hitler and the prospect of war with Germany becoming an ever likely possibility, it was deemed prudent to evacuate children from major British cities – Operation Pied Piper – and this would be principally carried out by the railways.

Plans were made and on 1 September 1939, three days before war was declared, a million children were moved from cities to host families in the country; it was the largest movement of people in British history. No fewer than 2,000 trains left from London.

To avoid trains being seen from the air, during black-out hours no lights were to be shown externally, and thus windows had to be screened and blue 15-watt bulbs fitted to offer minimum illumination. Carriage windows were covered in mesh so that if they were shattered by a bomb blast, glass shards would not injure passengers. It was very tempting for small children and others with a curious nature to pick at the mesh to determine how firmly it was attached. Platform lighting was limited to blue electric lights, or enclosed gas lamps below verandas. Coloured light signals were fitted with long hoods, and anti-glare sheets were fixed between a locomotive cab and its tender to obscure firebox glow, which made the footplate very hot.

The outbreak of war on 3 September 1939 caused great changes, one of the first being that, returning to school, I found that the class had doubled in size with lots of new faces and strange accents – belonging to children who had been evacuated to Bath, some from areas expected to be bombed and others whose fathers worked for the Admiralty. Nationwide, up to a million children were evacuated to the country.

If an evacuated child had worn-out shoes or clothes, a teacher would ask if another child could supply replacements.

As there were insufficient empty houses in Bath for all the Admiralty employees and their families, they had to be billeted with existing households. At times, this caused friction when the billetees and the original family did not see eye to eye, although when just one person was billeted, it was much easier.

NOTICE TO PASSENGERS

AIR RAID PRECAUTIONS

DURING AN AIR RAID :—

1. Close all windows and ventilators and pull down the blinds as a protection against flying glass.

2. If danger seems imminent, lie on the floor.

3. Never leave the train between stations unless so requested by a railway official.

4. Do not touch any outside part of a coach if a gas attack is suspected.

DURING BLACKOUT HOURS :—

1. KEEP ALL BLINDS DRAWN.

2. KEEP ALL WINDOWS SHUT except when necessary to lower them to open doors.

3. MAKE CERTAIN the train has stopped AT A PLATFORM and that you alight on the PLATFORM side.

4. WHEN LEAVING THIS COMPARTMENT, close windows, lower blinds again and close the door quickly.

Second World War railway posters.

To help restrict travel and leave the railways freer to move troops and evacuees, five days after the outbreak of war, football league games were suspended, although friendly competitive games, which did not involve so much nationwide travel, continued.

As the many bombing raids expected did not occur, many of the evacuees had returned home by Christmas 1939.

As there was a real threat of gas bombs being dropped, gas masks were issued and had to be carried to school daily, poor children carrying them in the cardboard box in which they were supplied, but others buying something more substantial. Periodically, teachers would inspect the masks to check that there were no holes and, if there were, they sent them to a depot for repair to be returned later that day. The local Air Raid Precaution (ARP) warden also came round to inspect the families' masks. Young children had special masks, not unlike Mickey Mouse in appearance, so they were given this name in order to make them less frightening.

The ARP wardens, together with the police, were also responsible for checking that no lights were showing after sunset which would have alerted the Luftwaffe that there was something below worth attacking. In addition, if the Luftwaffe could identify places, they were able to navigate better. It was highly embarrassing to hear a warden outside your home yell, 'Put that light out!' because as well as endangering yourself, you were endangering your neighbours. Before putting on a light, you had to ensure that a room was properly blacked out using extra thick curtains, hanging blankets or ground sheets at the windows, or fixing wooden frames covered with corrugated card. Churches, which had extra-large windows that were impractical to black out, moved their evening services forwards into daylight hours.

As there were no longer any streetlights and vehicles had to have their headlights masked and were permitted only one headlight, travelling on the roads was dangerous and during the first four months of the blackout, nearly 4,000 were killed on the roads. When going out at night you tried to wear something white, or light, in order to be as visible as possible. The parts of vehicles or posts likely to be struck were also painted white. When hailing a bus, you were supposed to shine your torch on to yourself and certainly not flash it into the driver's eyes as this would have affected his night vision for quite a few seconds. One great benefit of the blackout was that even in towns and cities, you could once again see and enjoy the stars in the night sky.

Apart from bombs actually destroying buildings, the blast from them could be fatal because of shards of glass from broken windows acting like flying daggers. In order to avoid this danger, windows were covered with netting, or a criss-cross of brown sticking paper which prevented glass from a shattered window flying about.

Large cities that expected to be bombed were protected by barrage balloons. Looking rather like flying elephants, these were held in place by cables which could slice the wing off an enemy plane thus forcing the enemy to fly above the balloons at a level which made accurate bombing more difficult. These balloons were filled from cylinders brought by a lorry and trailer, and provided something new for road spotters to observe.

One day in Portishead, I noticed some strange erections looking rather like pillar boxes placed intermittently along the pavement. On inquiry, I was told that in an air raid they burnt oil to produce smoke to conceal targets at the ports of Avonmouth and Portishead.

Children were interested in seeing the bases for fighters and bombers, which were springing up in many parts of the country, when they were out cycling or walking. Also of great interest were the RAF's extra-long 60-foot trailers called 'Queen Marys' which collected the remains of planes which had crashed.

Machine-gun posts made of sandbags sprang up to be ready in the event of an invasion and, as they were generally unoccupied, were ideal for boys to get into and pretend to shoot at the enemy. Main roads into a city had barriers of timber and barbed wire, along with holes in the road where, in the event of invasion, large inverted V-shaped pieces of metal called 'tank traps', sometimes made from old tram rails, could be placed to stop tanks and other army vehicles. As these barriers were permanently partly set up, they forced traffic in and out of the city to zigzag around them.

Everyone was warned of the dangers from incendiary bombs and taught how to deal with them. You picked one up – they were only about a foot long – with a long-handled shovel and placed it in a bucket of sand which you were required to have handy. If you were in a room which caught fire, you dropped to the floor where there was much less smoke and then crawled out. If the bomb had actually started a fire, you could use a stirrup pump to put it out.

The stirrup pump was like an inverted U, one arm being similar to a bicycle pump and the other arm simply a strong piece of metal, bent at its base so you could place a foot on it to keep it steady, this piece being rather like a stirrup. The pump was placed vertically inside a bucket of water, while the stirrup part remained outside. You then worked the pump and water squirted out of a hose which you placed on the fire. You could practise the technique by putting out a bonfire, which you were required to do when evening came on because it would have been against blackout regulations to keep it going. As heat rises, you were instructed to try to put a fire out while lying down so that there was less chance of catching fire yourself.

To guard against the shortage of firefighters in the event that a raid with incendiary bombs overcame the efforts of ordinary firemen, the AFS (Auxiliary Fire Service) was set up to assist them.

As the water mains may have been stopped by a bomb from an air raid, static water tanks were set up in various locations to supply water for firefighters. My house was about midway between the river and a tank and periodically firemen laid a hose between the two to top up the tank. On one occasion, the hose broke outside my house; water gushed out with considerable force and washed away soil from part of the flower bed before the crew was able to stop it.

We were warned about 'butterfly' bombs, so named because of the hinged outer shell which resembled opening wings. Because of their intriguing appearance, children were tempted to pick them up and, if they did, the bombs exploded.

One of my friends lived in a house on the outskirts of the city. One Monday, when I visited his house, he told me that he had something exciting to show me. He led me to the field adjacent to his home and told me that over the weekend soldiers, or the Home Guard, had built a gun emplacement from sandbags. That was not all he had to show me.

On the other side of his house was a garage to which he held the key. He took me in and – lo and behold – what was there but a gun. It was so big, it had to be supported on two wheels. What wonderful playthings and what scope for fun!

We were also warned of the danger of spies overhearing conversations which would give useful information to the enemy and were constantly reminded of this by posters announcing, 'Careless talk costs lives', 'Walls have ears' and 'Be like dad, keep mum'.

The father of one of my friends was in the Admiralty. One day while playing with him, I overheard his father on the telephone talking about a trip he was having to make to Ceylon (Sri Lanka). My friend's father reminded me that I should tell no one about his sailing as it could have been fatal had a German U-boat intercepted it. I didn't even tell my parents.

Air-raid shelters sprang up: some were of brick with a concrete roof, while others were merely roofed trenches. Several times, when returning from school, the air-raid siren sounded and I used a public shelter. Initially, when the air-raid siren sounded while at school, we sheltered beneath our desks, but a little later, arrangements were made for us to be dispersed in groups of six or so into houses near the school so that if bombs had fallen fewer children would have been killed. My junior school was situated in an area which would have been a prime target because within a few hundred yards of it were situated a large engineering works, a gas works, railway yard and a printing press.

My father strengthened our cellar for use as a shelter, but others used space under the staircase or a Morrison table shelter, which was a steel table with mesh sides that you could take refuge under. Some erected an Anderson shelter in their garden; this was a curved sheet of corrugated iron covered with soil.

In the countryside, large, flat fields had stones piled up at intervals to prevent enemy troops from landing, either by plane or glider.

School dinners were not provided until just after the start of the war. They were set up to supply meals for children who may have had both parents engaged in war work and who were thus unable to cook them a midday meal. The price was fivepence for each meal. Initially, schools didn't have their own kitchens; food was delivered in containers from a central kitchen elsewhere. These were made of aluminium and were double-walled to retain the heat. When the meals were delivered to the school gate, school monitors collected the containers and carried them to the classroom which was doubling as a dining room. This was unfortunate for children who had to use it in the afternoon for it stank of cabbage or whatever else had been eaten.

As buses and trams were often literally packed full of passengers who blocked the view of the platform of a busy conductor collecting fares, to save time taken to get a view of the platform to 'ring off' after a stop, volunteer auxiliary conductors were introduced for this task. 'Uncollected fare' boxes were also fixed by the platform.

In contrast to pre-war days when seeing a plane was unusual, they became an everyday sight. When coming out of my back door one day, I remember looking up and seeing a low-flying Spitfire with its pilot smiling and waving to me as I waved back.

On Saturday mornings, my friends and I, armed with large cardboard boxes, visited all the neighbouring houses collecting salvage. This was any scrap metal and included tins, cardboard, bottles, rags and paper which we carried to the back lane where it was collected the following week by a council lorry. Being 'green' is by no means a late twentieth-century invention. We did our bit to help the war effort. 'Make do and mend' was another familiar poster and we were expected to make our clothes last as long as possible. Although quite a few families had a sewing machine, which was a great help in making and repairing clothes, not every family could afford one.

Make-up became scarce during the war so older teenagers made their own. Beetroot was chopped, boiled, mashed and strained to extract the dye which could be painted on as lipstick. Skin could be treated with a foundation of calamine lotion before the application of cornflour starch, while black boot polish replaced mascara.

As German U-boats threatened food supplies from abroad, 'Dig for Victory' posters encouraged people to grow more food for themselves. Some particularly patriotic folk even sacrificed their lawns to help the war effort. Potatoes, lettuces, cabbage, carrots and beetroot were planted. Small children sowed the word 'Freedom' in mustard and cress, ate it and then planted the word 'Victory'.

Allotments were eagerly sought. This working of the land, apart from being good for the country, was good for the people. We got plenty of exercise in the open air. Sections of public parks were dug up to provide allotments, as were railway cuttings and embankments. One allotment holder, annoyed that someone on a neighbouring plot repeatedly stole water from his tank, ended the practice by putting weedkiller in the water. During the summer holidays, older children were encouraged to camp on farms and help to bring in the harvest because some of the farm workers had joined the forces.

Although before the war, some people had kept rabbits and hens, many more did so during the war in order to supplement their food quotas. This led to rationing of hen food, although rationing did not actually begin until January 1940. Pig food bins (which were actually just dustbins) were placed at intervals along roads and householders were encouraged to put their food waste into them. In fact, you could be fined for putting food waste in your own dustbin. The waste was collected by the council, boiled and sold to local pig keepers. Some people got together and formed a pig club. They bought a pig and fattened it up to eventually eat. To supplement the meat ration, many people kept rabbits; any children looking after them had to be warned that the rabbits were to eat and not kept as pets.

The Second World War had its effect on farming life. In the quest to provide more home-grown food, pastures on hills that were centuries old were ploughed for cereal crops, artificial fertiliser having to be used to produce a crop on stony ground. Wild-flower-rich hay meadows were ploughed and hedges and walls removed to create large fields which could be more easily worked by machinery.

Fish was not rationed but was in short supply and so was in great demand. While waiting to be served in a shop, it was much fairer to form an orderly queue so that those who arrived first would be dealt with first. Queues became so common that some people joined a queue and then asked what it was for! Queues were seen outside cinemas and at bus stops, but being first in a queue at a bus stop didn't guarantee you a place on the bus because on many occasions I can remember a bus was already filled with passengers at the terminus. Those at the first stop after the terminus would then watch it pass by. Those people who lived perhaps 2 miles from a town and wanted to use an intercity bus often found at rush hours that buses would not stop because they were full. The only solution was to catch a bus 2 miles into the town where the bus route started, but this added to your travel time and also to the cost.

As stopping and starting used more fuel than just going along at a normal pace, the distance between some bus stops was lengthened early on in the war in order to save fuel.

Oranges were not readily available during the war and thus people were encouraged to get vitamin C from rose hips for it was claimed they had seven times more vitamin C than an orange. I remember one autumn seeing a briar loaded with hips and busily set about filling all my trouser and jacket pockets with them, but there were still some left. Where could I put them? I tucked as many as I could into my socks.

Once I was home, my mother cut the hips in half, the hairs and seeds were scraped out, or the whole hips minced, then they were boiled and strained through muslin. You could then make syrup, jam or purée.

We were encouraged to make stinging nettle soup as well as to cook dandelions which, we were assured, tasted like spinach, a vegetable with which I was not much enamoured. Wild meat off the ration could also be had, such as wood pigeon, rook, rabbit and hare.

The cinema became very popular during the war; most people went once or twice weekly because, in addition to the entertainment on offer, you also saw moving pictures about the war. This helped to amplify the situation since newspapers were unable to supply much information because, due to the shortage of imported newsprint, they were only allowed to have four pages.

To help the war effort, children, even juniors, knitted gloves, mittens, scarves, socks and balaclavas for the forces; they made up parcels with other small items to show that they cared for those fighting for their freedom.

'Economise' was a key word during the war. I remember a brush company advertised its products by putting a pencil economiser through each door. It consisted of a 5-inch length of tin tube, slightly smaller in diameter than the pencil stub which you thrust into it. A girl with whom I played had been given a pencil with her name printed on it and when the economiser arrived through her letter box, she pushed her quite long pencil into it covering up her name. When the person who gave her the pencil was coming to tea, her parents knew that she might be asked to show it and so told her to take it out of the economiser. It was pushed in so tightly that she could only take it out by splitting it completely open – so there was no economy.

The underground stone quarries at Corsham were made into an ammunition depot in the late thirties because war with Germany had become a real possibility by that time. A lot of manpower was required for this and, in 1939, some of this was provided from Bristol. A convoy of old buses, the likes of which had not been seen in Bath for many years, conveyed the workers and provided an interesting sight for transport enthusiasts. It was deemed uneconomic to employ drivers to take the buses to Corsham and then wait for hours while doing nothing before driving them back to Bristol; those workers who held a bus driving licence drove the workers to and fro.

Memorable Events in the 1930s

1930: Sir Henry Seagrave killed on Lake Windermere while attempting to exceed 100mph on water, 13 June. He averaged 98.6mph on two runs before being killed on his third run. He was the first person to hold both the land- and water-speed records simultaneously; airship R. 101 destroyed in France on first flight to India, forty-eight lives lost, 5 October.

1931: New Road Traffic Act came into force, 1 January; opening of Zoological Gardens at Whipsnade, 23 May; great floods in China, 4 million homes destroyed and 23 million people affected, 5 August.

1932: Sydney Harbour Bridge opened, 19 March; Buckfast Abbey consecrated, 25 August.

1933: The German Reichstag set on fire, 27 February; a Soviet balloon ascended 19,000 metres, 30 September; the *Discovery II* left England on an Antarctic expedition, 21 October.

1934: Earthquake in North India killed 7,252, 15 January; the *Queen Mary* launched, 26 September; Herr Dollfuss, the Austrian chancellor, assassinated by Austrian Nazis, 25 July.

1935: Earthquake in Formosa killed 3,185 and injured 10,630, 21 April; Silver Jubilee of King George V's accession, 6 May; 30,000 lives lost in earthquake at Quetta, 31 May; British offer of a piece of Somaliland Territory to avert the Abyssinian War refused by Italy, 27 June; Queen Astrid of the Belgians killed in motoring accident near Lucerne, 29 August; outbreak of war between Italy and Abyssinia, 3 October.

1936: Death of King George V and accession of King Edward VIII, 20 January; Repudiation of the Locarno Treaty by Germany, 7 March; Emperor of Abyssinia fled from Addis Ababa to Bath and settled 200 yards from the author's home, 2 May; civil war broke out in Spain, 18 July; Foundation stone of Guildford Cathedral laid, 22 May; Crystal Palace destroyed by fire, 30 November; King Edward VIII abdicated, 10 December; Duke of York succeeded his brother as King George VI, 12 December.

1937: King George VI and Queen Elizabeth crowned, 12 May; the salaries of MPs raised from £400 to £600 p.a., 22 June.

1938: Singapore naval base opened, 14 February; Austria annexed by Germany, 12 March; cholera in India killed 14,000, 18 June; the *Queen Mary* gained the Blue Riband for making the fastest west-to-east crossing in three days, twenty hours, forty-two minutes, 14 August; the largest liner, the *Queen Elizabeth*, launched, 27 September; Munich Agreement between Chamberlain, Daladier, Hitler and Mussolini signed, 29 September.

1939: Great Britain recognises General Franco's Government, 27 February; Bohemia and Moravia annexed by Hitler, 16 March; Chamberlain warns Germany against domination by force, 17 March; anti-Polish press campaign begun by Germany, 28 March; Spanish Civil War ends, 1 April; Italy seizes Albania,

7 April; conscription introduced in Great Britain, 27 April; Hitler denounces the Anglo-German Naval Agreement and the Polish Non-Aggression Treaty, 28 April; Italy and Germany sign pact, 2 May; Great Britain signs defensive agreement with Turkey, 12 May; Italy and Germany sign pact, 22 May; France and Turkey sign defensive agreement, 22 May; Anglo-Polish treaty signed, 25 May; German–Soviet pact signed, 23 August; Poland invaded by Germany, 1 September; compulsory military service for all British men aged 18 to 41, 2 September; Britain declares war on Germany 11.00 a.m., France at war with Germany from 5 p.m., 3 September; British liner *Athenia* sunk by German submarine; the RAF raid the Kiel Canal entrance and bomb German warships, 4 September; Germans advance into Silesia and the Polish Corridor, 5 September; first enemy air raid on Britain, Allied planes bomb Saar objectives, 6 September; Russia mobilises, 8 September; Russian troops on Polish border, 10 September; British troops on French soil, 11 September; Poland collapses, Russian and German troops meet near Brest; HMS *Courageous* sunk with loss of 515 lives, 17 September; German–Soviet pact signed approving partition of Poland, 29 September; *Royal Oak* sunk with loss of 810 lives, 14 October; German bombers raid Rosyth and the Firth of Forth, 16 October; *Admiral Graf Spee* is scuttled at entrance to Montevideo harbour, 17 December.